AF580217

Before You Were Everything

Before You Were Everything

REFLECTIONS ON
FINDING LOVE, LEGACY,
AND BECOMING
IN A LIFE REWRITTEN

Mya Fort-Marshall

Before You Were Everything: Reflections on Finding Love, Legacy, and Becoming in a Life Rewritten

©2026 Mya Fort-Marshall. All Rights Reserved. No part of this publication may be reproduced, stored in a retrieval system or transmitted in any form by any means electronic, mechanical, or photocopying, recording or otherwise without the permission of the author.

For more information, please contact:
Amplify Publishing, an imprint of Amplify Publishing Group
620 Herndon Parkway, Suite 220
Herndon, VA 20170
info@amplifypublishing.com

Library of Congress Control Number: 2025925957

CPSIA Code: PRV0226A

ISBN-13: 979-8-90026-007-5

Printed in the United States

For the women who raised me, the sons who remade me, and the friends who carried me when I forgot how to move forward.

This book is for anyone who ever needed proof that the messy, beautiful middle is still holy ground.

CONTENTS

AUTHOR'S NOTE

This is not a self-help book.

There's no five-step plan. No vision board exercise. No chapter on "finding your why."

You will not be transformed by page 127.

You might not even be sure what genre this is.

Because it isn't a memoir either. Not exactly.

Some of these stories are absolutely true.

Some have been lovingly exaggerated for dramatic effect—because healing is important, but so is entertainment.

So if you're wondering, *Did that really happen?* The answer is: probably. But also, maybe not. And honestly . . . does it matter?

What matters is that it feels true.

Growing up among storytellers, I've learned that what matters is not just the telling; it's about the landing. Not just cracking jokes or spilling tea, but dropping something that sticks to your ribs. To offer up pieces of myself—the songs, the side dishes, the heartbreaks and hallelujahs, and toss all them into the fire we gather around. Because story is communion. It feeds. It flames. It binds. And if we are lucky, it also makes us laugh with our mouths full.

Because this one is not mine alone. I have kneaded ancestral blessings and ancient griefs into the bread we're about to break. I have spiked our brew with brutal truth and sweetened it with belly laughs. In telling it, I hand it to you, a re-collection of fabled facts passed across the fire, meant to warm your palms and maybe light up a corner of yourself you thought was hidden.

This book isn't a manual.

It's a mirror.

It's a soft place to land.

It's a late-night phone call with a friend who knows how to hold your contradictions.

The one who'll let you cry, cuss, laugh, spiral a little—and then remind you who the hell you are.

This book won't fix your life.

But it might help you hear yourself more clearly.

And maybe—just maybe—it'll offer a little companionship as you become the person you already are.

So . . . hi.

I've been saving your spot, and I am so glad you finally made it.

Let's begin.

PART I
Who Raised You—Pirates?

IF THIS CHAPTER HAD A FLAVOR

Grandma's butter rolls

IF THIS CHAPTER HAD A SOUNDTRACK

"THE HORSES"	RICKIE LEE JONES
"ADORE"	PRINCE
"NEVER TOO MUCH"	LUTHER VANDROSS
"CAUGHT UP IN THE RAPTURE"	ANITA BAKER
"FOR THE LOVE OF MONEY"	THE O'JAYS
"HIS EYE IS ON THE SPARROW"	WHITNEY HOUSTON (LAURYN HILL AND TANYA BLOUNT VERSION)

I've been called all kinds of things by men trying to pin down whatever it is they were feeling in my presence. At this point, I expect it. So when a could-be suitor, exasperated by my blunt tongue and quick wit, once asked, "Who raised you—pirates?" All I could do was smile to myself.

Oh, sir. You have no idea.

If Amazonia were real, its coordinates would lead you to 875 S. Jackson Ave., in San Jose, California. A modest house built in 1961, the kind you might expect to see in a sitcom rerun, if not for the paint: a sage green that flirted with neon, depending on the light. Lawn clipped tight. Bushes neatly trimmed. A tree out front demanding to be climbed and a pale-yellow Toyota pickup sitting in the driveway: my grandfather's pride.

But the house, and everything in it? He'd tell you that was his wife's domain.

Neatly nestled on a busy street, within walking distance to anything you might need, my physical universe was small—however, my universe of imagination was not bound to geography, gender, or the restrictive realm of "impossibility."

Inside, it was a different world. A whole nation unto itself.

A nation of Fort women who made 1,216 square feet of wood paneling and wicker furniture feel palatial. My grandmother's house. The nexus and nucleus of my early childhood.

My mother—Candice—is one of eleven children, three boys and eight girls. And while my grandfather and uncles did their best to control the weather, those eight sisters were hurricane-force winds.

Beautiful. Blunt. Brilliant in ways that bent time. They sidestepped gender norms and answered only to the logic of what worked.

They were glamorous and practical. Sharp-tongued and open-hearted. The Fort women made *impossible* look routine.

I watched them raise babies and hell, earn degrees, fix bathroom sinks, curse creatively, lead choirs, cook dinner, and pour a drink without spilling an ounce of dignity.

Nothing captured that better than my grandmother's butter rolls. Pillowy dough, layered in butter and sugar, traditionally baked in sweet milk. She made them her own way. Instead of baking the rolls in sweet milk, she waited until they crisped in the oven, then poured the cream over the top. That way, the edges stayed strong while the sauce soaked in, bite by bite. Comfort disguised as dessert. Love as sweetness. That was my grandmother. That was the Fort women: crisp edges softened with sugar and cream. Practical hands making magic out of whatever was around, ordinary ingredients turned extraordinary because of who held them.

Our values were rooted in presence, in honesty, in survival. These were women who came of age in the sixties and seventies, who loved *Grease* and the Jackson 5. They understood the cost of racism and the power of feminism, not from being broken, but from being relentlessly aware. Middle class meant we weren't fighting for food, but it also meant my aunts had the time and the audacity to think, to question, to name what privilege gave and what it withheld.

And they were funny. Funny in a way that made the whole block lean in. Funny in a way that healed everything, from loss to systemic failures. If a joke could be made, we were laughing before the punchline, but if a joke shouldn't be made—even better. That was a dare we simply couldn't resist.

In our house, love didn't always sound sweet. But it always sounded loud. Nicknames were sacred and savage and wildly specific.

They called my mom "Witchy Poo"—probably after some failed exorcism following a stretch of nights with Ouija boards. Growing up, Mom hid books on voodoo underneath floorboards like porn. Not because she was devoted to the practice, but because she was restless with questions the church couldn't answer. She searched for something that resonated with what she knew in her heart to be true. That search led her through Afro-Caribbean rituals and Eastern philosophies, until she landed in the Tao.

My Auntie Arnita? "Leak Leak." She wet the bed as a kid, and that name chased her into adulthood. My Auntie Carolyn? "Red." Light-skinned and radiant. My Uncle Sherman? "Double B." (Short for "Double Black.") And me?

"Muff."

I wish I could say mine was short for something. Instead, it's a popular reference to . . . exactly what you think it is. My Uncle Thaddaeus took one look at the puff of curls on my newborn head and said, "Her head looks like a muff of hair." And for those of you wondering what that is, well, you must have been raised by polite and proper stock.

From that moment on, I was Muff. Muffy. Muffarooroo. Muffaletta. It never felt mean. It felt like mine.

When you're raised like that, you don't question it.

You don't think twice about names that would land a parent in a conference room today. Because in my house, those names were layered in love and seasoned with sarcasm.

In my family, emotional sensitivity wasn't well understood—and very rarely embraced.

Tears were met with suspicion. Confusion. Disappointment.

And so, I evolved. From sensitive to stoic. Unmoving. I didn't just learn to regulate my emotions, I learned to tuck them away. Repression dressed itself up as resilience. I embraced it. And I was praised for it.

Becoming less sensitive never felt like a loss.

Back then, it felt like a superpower.

I didn't even realize how different my world was until one day in kindergarten, when we were reciting nursery rhymes.

Ladybug, ladybug, fly away home . . .

When we got to that line, I said it loud and proud: "Your house is on fire, your children are burned."

My teacher looked at me horrified.

I blinked, confused. That's how I'd always heard it.

Because in my family, that's how it went. My aunts had swapped "gone" for "burned" years ago—because their dark humor found it funnier that way. It was twisted. It was dramatic. It was *them*.

And to me, it was normal.

That moment taught me something I didn't have words for yet: Other people were playing a completely different game. One where "burned children" wasn't funny. One where your nickname didn't reference pubic hair.

I idolized my aunties. Every single one of them.

And when you grow up in the presence of women like that—women who could run households, build furniture, and rock a red lip in the same breath—gradeschoolers are . . . disappointing.

In first grade, my teacher was concerned. She pulled my mom aside one afternoon, worried that I didn't play with the other kids at recess. I didn't run or scream or chase. I walked slow laps. I chatted with the yard aides. I kept company with my thoughts.

My mom listened patiently, then told her, "She prefers adults."

She wasn't wrong.

It wasn't that I couldn't make friends. Other seven-year-olds simply couldn't compete. Not when I had a front row-seat to Auntie Red's stories, punctuated by my mom's laughter and my other aunties' commentary seasoning the plot.

By the time I reached this age, I had been exposed to more humor, heat, heartbreak, and brilliance at the kitchen table than most adults get in a year. So no, I wasn't all that interested in hopscotch.

That teacher's concern was sweet. But unnecessary.

Because I had an audience with some of the best people I've ever known.

My grandmother's house was always full. Of people. Of food. Of music. Of presence.

Her children returned when life asked too much of them. That meant I got to live with my aunts—at least for some time.

My mom left me in my grandmother's care when I was two. She was just twenty-two herself, divorced from my dad and terrified of a new boyfriend who came with an angry fist that left her with a lonely black eye. She had the sense to know that once was enough. Fear carried her clear across the country to Massachusetts, somewhere safe. Somewhere he couldn't find her.

My musician dad was on tour, but between cities he made time for visits. He laughed with my aunts, traded jokes with my grandfather, and fit right in at my grandma's house. He was a friend to Jackson Ave., and always a friend to my mom—the kind of friend who flew his three-year-old daughter across the country to Boston, just to soften the ache between mother and child for a few precious days.

A couple of years later, when the coast was clear, she came back. At the end of the long hallway, in the last of three bedrooms, Mom and I curled into bunk beds and shared our secrets, mother and daughter folding into something that also felt like sisters . . . And though she eventually moved out on her own, she let me stay with my grandparents in the only home I had ever known. Looking back, it was always me and Grams. Along with Grandpa Fort, we were the constants. Everyone else orbited.

That house offered more than shelter. It gave me a lens. It showed me who I came from. It showed me what womanhood could look like.

It wasn't always easy. But it was rich and riotous and sometimes raunchy. And it was mine.

Through the revolving door of that home, I collected lessons from the women who passed through—some for years, some for a season, some just for Thanksgiving dinner.

Each of them left something with me.

From Auntie Melinda, I learned resilience.

She wasn't the oldest by birth order, but in our grandmother's house, she carried elder-daughter energy like a birthright. She returned as an adult with her two daughters—not because she was lost, but because she was building something. A life that wasn't defined by struggle, but by structure. By strategy. By sourdough.

She worked long hours, then went to night school. Grams would've been more than happy to handle dinner, and on nights when classes let out way past our bedtime, she did. But most nights, my aunt came home exhausted—and put together a meal before even thinking about sitting down to rest. Every plate, no matter what she cooked, was served with a single slice of sourdough, buttered and toasted to perfection in the broiler. Her quiet signature at the end of the day.

It was never about the bread. It was the ritual. The reliability. The soft landing she created for her girls . . . and for me.

Then, just like that, one day she was gone. Not from our lives, but from the house. She had hustled her way into a new zip code. A quieter one. She didn't just move out.

She moved forward.

From Auntie Arnita, I learned persistence.

Not the polite kind. Not the "hashtag productivity" kind.

But the kind that bulldozes through red tape and doesn't wait for permission.

The woman could maneuver around a return policy like it was a sport. She had a workaround for everything, and if she didn't—she made one up and made it stick. Once Arnita had a goal, it was happening. Period. She didn't manifest it. She barreled straight through it.

Bold and unapologetic as she was, she also gave grace. Because as much as her presence sometimes demanded forgiveness—she offered it freely. Without ego. Without drama. Just presence and a clean slate.

And she was funny. I spent many nights up way past my bedtime, howling with laughter at her stories or watching VHS tapes of Luther Vandross concerts. She taught me how to play Spades before it should've been legal. We didn't gamble with money, just pride. We always kept score. By fifth grade I could count *books* (the number of hands you commit to winning) and call out a *renege* (when somebody plays a suit they already swore they didn't have). I knew exactly when to play the big and little joker.

When I finally threw my cards down, I'd channel the righteous fury of a grown woman who'd just discovered her paycheck was short. At nine years old, I was ready to teach that table accountability. I got that spark from Auntie Arnita. And even though she warned us of her limits and authority—"I like kids, but I *don't play*"—I always felt like an equal in her eyes.

We called her Mama Nita, because that's exactly what she was. A mama to us. To her nieces and nephews. To the kids she didn't birth but helped raise.

When she moved out of Grams's house and into her own apartment, I often followed her home, sometimes for entire summers—like it was instinct. Because being around her felt like freedom. Like being seen without being babied. Like being shaped by someone who didn't always show love the conventional way—but always made you feel it.

From my mom, Candice, I learned what love looks like.

I was ten. It was Easter morning. We were sharing the top bunk of a twin bed in my grandparents' house. She'd usually sleep on the bottom, but that morning she squeezed in next to me. I welcomed the closeness. She was Rosie the Riveter and Wonder Woman rolled into one. I hoped her superpowers were contagious, and nestled even closer.

"Open your eyes," she whispered. And when I did—there it was.

A bunny. A real, live bunny sitting on her chest.

Joy. Then panic. *My grandparents are going to kill us.*

She looked calm. Confident. Unbothered. Already dressed in her favorite button-fly 501s, curls spilling over the pillow.

I whispered, "Who's gonna tell Grandma?"

Because while my mom was wild magic, my grandmother was guarded peace, the kind concealing a pistol with a silencer. I put on the pink lace dress my grandmother helped me pick out. Slipped into the shoes. Grabbed the matching purse. Went to church.

While we were gone, my mom stayed behind. She slipped into *her* sanctuary, the nearby hardware store, and came back with two-by-fours and cage wire, everything she needed to build a bunny hutch. That was the deal: If we wanted to keep it, she had to build it.

By the time we returned, it was done. Sturdy. Beautiful. Perfect.

She was sitting in a lawn chair, beer in hand, smiling in the sun. Relaxed in a way that made her spirituality radiate from her like sunshine . . . it was love you could see.

As for the bunny? I wish I had some touching childhood memory of raising it into old age.

That Easter gift was a delight, a memory of bold love propped up by cage wire, two-by-fours, and responsibility. But once I began to lose interest, another family impulse won out. One day the bunny was there; the next I was told it had "run away." But here's the thing: In my family, a small prey mammal wouldn't just *run away.* Let's just say my very down-home Texan grandpa had developed an early taste for possum, raccoon, and yes . . . rabbit. Odds were it didn't escape. Odds were, it was seasoned. I never asked. Some truths are better left implied.

Youthful novelties may fade, but the boldfaced love animating my mother's soft surprise never did. She may have skipped that Easter worship service, but each nail she hammered into those wooden boards was a prayer. Love, for my mom, didn't need a sermon or a steeple. She didn't reject God. She just didn't outsource Him. She didn't contain Him in a book or under a steeple.

Grandma took me to church and taught me that God was love. But that day, my mom taught me what love looks like. How to shoot arrows of whimsy on an Easter morning, then take responsibility for how they land.

For the first twelve years of my life, I was raised in my grandparents' high-traffic house on South Jackson Ave. In seventh grade, a shift in district lines landed me at a middle school notorious for fights and chaos. On my second day, a boy walked into class with a sawed off shotgun tucked in his backpack. That was it. My mom and grandmother agreed it was time for a district shift of our own.

So I moved in with my mom—the person I most aspired to be like.

My grandma taught me how to be a lady. My mom taught me how to push the boundaries of that definition.

Those two women—those two houses—could not have been more different.

My grandmother, rooted in faith and function, shaped me with structure. My mother, free-spirited and fierce, shaped me with imagination.

Between them, I learned how to pray and how to protest.

How to stand still and how to fly.

That paradox—holy and hippie, structured and strange—shaped me. It made me curious instead of judgmental.

I didn't realize it then, but being raised in a space that

held both incense and gospel . . . it gave me a gift.

A blueprint for how to hold contradiction without crumbling.

And that's the real work of growing up, isn't it? Learning to translate all those impressions and sensations inside yourself. Learning what to carry and what to release. Understanding that some customs hold you . . . and some hold you back. Even the cultures we love must evolve. Especially the ones we inherit.

Culture is powerful, but it is not perfect. It's a starting point—not a final draft. It's a story we get to edit. Those women who raised me—the woman they raised me to be—never fail to raise eyebrows. They are unlike any others I've known, and their imprint is the kind of extraordinary that feels equal parts maddening and majestic, a kaleidoscope of contradictions that refuse to conform.

If I could go back and whisper anything to my twenty-something self—the one who tried to blend in, to soften her edges, to get it "right"—I'd say this:

You were already enough. How dare you try to tame the glorious weird your five-year-old self so thoughtfully curated?

And to my forty-something self?

Welcome back.

The magic was never in "fitting in." It was in remembering who the hell you've always been.

So when that man asked me, "Who raised you—pirates?" Obviously, I said, "Yes."

PART II

Becoming on Brace Ave.

IF THIS CHAPTER HAD A FLAVOR

"Muffaletta" grilled cheese

IF THIS CHAPTER HAD A SOUNDTRACK

"PEOPLE EVERYDAY"............ARRESTED DEVELOPMENT

"KEEP YA HEAD UP"............2PAC

"'93 'TIL INFINITY"............SOULS OF MISCHIEF

"GIRLS JUST WANT TO HAVE FUN"............CYNDI LAUPER

"DOO WOP (THAT THING)"............LAURYN HILL

We moved to Brace Ave. in Willow Glen the year everything started to shift.

It was the same apartment complex where my Aunt Melinda and my cousins lived, and it offered something between a soft landing and a restart.

The apartment itself was modest: two bedrooms, first floor, with popcorn ceilings and hardwood floors that remembered every footstep. But it was ours. A place where the fridge was full of condiments and religiously lacking in protein, and the counter always had a note from Mom. The kind every nineties latchkey kid knew by heart. A to-do list with chores I never touched at Gram's house. (I could not tell you how to mop a floor, and the one time I tried Ajax, Mom was not amused. The gritty floors didn't seem impressed either.) Each note ended with instructions and a few dollars for dinner.

I went from Sunshine Band and fully prepped after-school snacks to Hermann Hesse novels and dinner money left on the counter. From peanut butter and jelly sandwiches with the crust cut off to brie and olives. From forks to chopsticks—because my mom decided they were all we needed. And honestly? They were.

Mom and I also shared a love for reading. Grandma, who worked as a teacher's aide, taught me to read at four, so by second or third grade I was already tearing through novels. My mom kept a massive bookshelf, full of books Grams probably wouldn't approve of. They were philosophical, loaded with questions about everything I'd been told was true. I devoured them all: Maya Angelou, Daniel Quinn, John Kennedy Toole, and everything in between.

Willow Glen was different. A polished little suburb of San Jose that looked like a Hallmark town on its best behavior. It was whiter than the east side, quieter, cleaner. The kind of place where people watered their lawns before 8 a.m., and you felt safe walking alone at night.

Mom enrolled me in the local middle school. I was in seventh grade, still someone who liked school and believed in fresh starts.

I made friends quickly. Between the cousins upstairs and the kids who drifted in and out of our apartment like it had a revolving door, I managed to recreate the traffic I'd grown up with at my grandmother's house.

After school, my days followed a new routine. It looked and felt like this:

I turn the knob on our front door and it opens easily. We hardly ever lock it. It could be our "one-love" sensibilities or the fact that we live in a low-crime neighborhood, but we're unbothered by risk. The door is always open. That's just how it's always been.

I skip inside, wearing clothes that don't belong to me. My mom doesn't have many rules, but she's made it very clear: Don't wear her clothes. Still, I pass the black-and-white photo of Bob Marley on the wall and make a beeline for her room.

We are artists. That much is obvious.

There's a canvas leaning against her bed—her naked torso sketched across it in charcoal. Her dresser is hand-painted, layered with images of Siddhartha, Hindu gods, and other spiritual symbols. Everything in her room feels curated by instinct. Chaotic. Divine.

But I don't linger. I head for the closet. It's already open, the track littered with shoes and accessories like it exploded in slow motion.

My mom wears jeans and white tees most days. But when she dresses up? She transforms. Her closet is a museum of vintage finds—sequined and beaded gowns that smell antique in the best way. They are heavy with memory. Dresses that demand backstories. I imagine the parties they once attended. The women they made feel seen. The weight of those decades stitched into every hem.

I hang the broom skirt I "borrowed" back in the closet, hoping she won't notice. She always does.

I slip into my own jeans and wander to the kitchen for a snack.

Now—the refrigerator isn't for beginners. At first glance, it looks empty. But we know better. I pull out a tub of tapenade, jam, a wedge of brie, a loaf of French bread, a butter knife, and . . . chopsticks. Of course.

A fridge like that teaches resourcefulness. Condiments become meals if you're curious enough. Sweet, salty, savory . . . a little improvisation, a little invention. That's how the Muffaletta Grilled Cheese was born: brie and apples tucked between my grandma's homemade peach jam and olive tapenade, grilled into something that tastes like contradiction but lands like truth. A sandwich born from chaos and curiosity, just like Brace Ave. itself.

Back in the living room, I sit cross-legged on the floor to assemble my snack. The bread tears easily, the olives are salty, the brie is soft and perfect. I twist the TV knob and land on a music video of Tupac's "Dear Mama." I hum along, a little offbeat, head nodding like prayer.

A few minutes later, my best friend, Thomas, walks in. No knock. No announcement. Just vibes. The door's always open, and that's all the invitation he needs.

Mouth full of bread and cheese, I greet him with a nod.

He heads to the kitchen. I hear the fridge door open. Then, after a beat, I hear him shout:

"Y'all never have anything to eat!"

He walks back in, slumps onto the couch like he lives here, and eyes my plate like it's alien fare.

I offer him some of my sandwich. Messy and sticky between fingers determined to devour this treat in record time. He considers it, amazed and amused, like I'd just held out a mud pie.

"Do you and your mom ever eat Black people food?"

I don't flinch.

I know what he means. I know what he's trying to ask. To him, this . . . doesn't look like the Black experience. But by then, I'd already decided I didn't need permission or consensus. My experience is Black because I am Black.

What other qualifying factors could there be?

There was this free love, leave-the-door-unlocked, everybody's-welcome kind of ease in those days.

Communal. Comfortable. Enshrouded in the kind of messy, beautiful warmth women create when they raise each other without realizing it.

I was still a strange kid—comfortable in clothes no one else wore, sharp-tongued but genuinely empathetic. And somehow, despite all the typical middle school mindset that tends to leave the weird kids out . . . I found friends.

Some were weird like me. Others were my opposite in almost every way. But they were mine.

Those same friends—the ones I made between seventh and twelfth grade— sustain me to this day.

Their presence both taught and affirmed me.

They let me be me, as much as young people know how. They taught me how to look out for myself in the world.

Because when you go around expecting things to just work out . . . it's usually because they always have.

At least, that was my experience. I was raised by women

who didn't just believe in me—they dared the world to *try me*. I didn't grow up with gentle affirmations or emotional processing. I grew up with backup. With doors unlocked, but eyes scanning for threats. With people who made it known: *If you come for her, you come for us.*

My Auntie Shermaine—nicknamed "BayBay," a lifelong role earned by being the youngest of the Fort sisters—was all fire and no brakes. She once threatened to fight a kid for being mean to me. And honestly? She meant it.

Her twin brother, my Uncle Sherman, was the opposite. Not a fighter at all. More of a lover. A pastor, actually. The kind of man who smells like cologne and conviction. But even he—quiet, spiritual, tender—would've reached for a little hell if it meant shielding me.

I didn't grow up thinking life was "fair."

I grew up knowing I was protected.

So I walked through the world expecting things to work out—not because I believed I was untouchable, but because I knew someone would always come for me. That there would be a way forward. That the story would end in my favor or, at the very least, with my feet firmly planted and some laughs in the telling.

I believed in happy endings because I lived them. Because every fall I took was followed by someone catching me.

Because even disappointment came with a soft landing—and usually, a silver lining attached.

That's what I knew.

But many of my friends?

They grew up in different realities. Realities where landmines weren't hypothetical. They moved through the world with instincts I didn't yet have. They showed me how to scan for danger on my own.

How to read a room. How to keep your guard up even when your heart is open.

In return . . . I hope I gave them a safe place to breathe. A bubble of their own, even if it was restricted to that small apartment on Brace.

The first day of freshman year, I met my long-lost sister, Tanesha.

Not lost in terms of DNA strands separated at birth, but in the way you don't realize you've been missing someone . . . until they show up.

She exuded confidence. Spoke to everyone. A Leo, wise beyond her years, determined not just to survive high school, but to enjoy it. Fully. Loudly. Boldly.

Tanesha carried adult responsibilities not because she chose to but because her life demanded the haul. And still, she danced through the weight of it all to a rhythm only she could hear.

Her story deserves its own spotlight, and one day she'll write the book it's owed. What matters here is that we found each other—and once we did, we were family.

We were wildly different. She was all sparkle and spice and side-eyes. I was quirky and soft and didn't quite belong to any category. We didn't share friends, and that's still true. Different interests, different circles, different lives. But none of that mattered.

Because what we shared ran deeper.

We shared secrets, inside jokes, and late-night talks that bent time. At various points in our lives, we shared rooms—including the one on Brace Ave. We shared a kind of *chosen* that didn't need to be spoken. It just was.

She taught me that love isn't about constant agreement; it's about showing up. It's presence. It's sticking around. Even when you don't understand each other. Especially then.

She showed me what it means to be loved without condition . . . and to offer that kind of love back.

I was my mom's only child, and my dad's other kids were out of reach by geography and circumstance. But when Tanesha showed up, she quickly became my mom's other daughter. And as I grew my chosen family, so did my mom, claiming each new child I brought home as one of her own.

Ferris and JoJo lived upstairs.

Melinda's girls. They weren't just cousins. They were sisters in all the ways that mattered. Chosen by blood, kept close by love.

They were both younger than me—JoJo by seven years, Ferris by three. And when you're a teenager, that kind of age gap feels like an ocean. They were always the "little cousins."

Then you grow up. At some point, suddenly, you realize you're standing on the same level. Same fears. Same questions. Same battle to make sense of who you are.

JoJo was a sprite. At eight, she was wild and mischievous—curious about everything, fearless about most things, and sharp as a scalpel.

She spoke the kind of honesty that made adults pause and kids cry. Honest in ways that sometimes made you flinch, but always made you better. She called out what didn't add up, even if it wasn't her business—especially then.

Even at thirty, that didn't change. It only deepened. Her honesty got sharper, but so did her wisdom. She still held up the mirror, but now she offered a tissue for the tears afterward. You couldn't hide around JoJo. She saw too much and loved too hard to let you settle for less than the truth.

Ferris was another story. Quieter. A sage, even as a child. By age twelve, she carried herself like someone who had seen it all. Someone who understood the stakes of being misunderstood. Intentional. Self-reflective. She watched everything. Took it all in like a scientist of human nature—observing, not judging. (Well, maybe judging a little.) She grounded into herself even when the world around her was spinning.

I've never met someone so quietly determined to live life on their own terms. Patient in her becoming. Ferris didn't just resist being molded; she simply never stepped into the clay. She was herself, and watching her grow into that without apology was its own kind of liberation.

Growing up between these two felt like sitting between fire and earth. JoJo pushed. Ferris anchored. And somewhere in that space, I found parts of myself.

They started as my little cousins. But the truth is . . . I still learned from them. That's the beauty of it.

They were younger, but I always looked to them to bring their gifts—because even then, I knew we were raising each other.

So when they called me "cousin" instead of *sister*, I felt a little cheated. Until Tanesha entered my life, and the universe finally corrected itself.

Life on Brace wasn't just shaped by the people living inside that apartment. It was also shaped by the neighbors and guests—and occasional intruders. In fact, nothing captures the spirit of that house better than *the hammer.*

At one point, I shared my bedroom with Tanesha and another one of my cousins, Juanita. Three teenage girls. One tiny room. And a house always crawling with other teenagers whose stays rarely came with a departure time. My mom did her best to never leave a kid out in the cold—figuratively or literally. So the door stayed open. And so did the floor, the couch, and the pantry.

Juanita was Thaddaeus's daughter—a month younger than me and almost a foot taller. She was stunning, over-makeupped, and on this particular day, determined not to mind her business.

After school, we saw a girl from our high school harassing a middle schooler over fundraiser candy. Juanita told her to "knock it off." That night, the girl called our house—furious. Said she was coming over.

So we waited. Stood in the street like idiots, full of

teenage bravado and false confidence.

Quick pause for context: I had never been in a fight before in my life. Not even a pushing-on-the-playground situation. I was a little naive about all the things that spelled danger. So when Hammer Girl reached into her backpack . . . I didn't flinch.

But Juanita and Tanesha? They *ran*. Immediately. Full sprint to the apartment like their feet already knew the ending.

It took me a second longer to catch up—mentally, emotionally, spiritually. And by the time I turned to follow . . . the door had closed behind them.

There we were.

Just me and Hammer Girl.

She looked me dead in the eye and pulled out . . . yes, a literal hammer.

So I said the first thing that came to mind: "Oh my god . . . your breath stinks."

She hit me. Hard on the side. *With a hammer.* My brain could not process what had just happened.

So I laughed. Loudly. Because that's what I'd been trained to do. In my family, all emotion, fear, sadness, anger, got remixed into laughter. It was our survival song.

My laughter left her confused and shaken, with nothing to do but go home. I was left with a bruise, deep and angry, and skin split right in the center of my left rib. Back in the house, when the adrenaline drained, the pain roared to life. By the time my mom came home from work, she was livid. She couldn't understand how our whole commune of teenagers had stood by while her pacifist daughter took a hammer to the ribs. As for the "commune"? They couldn't understand why I hadn't run faster.

I can laugh now, but the days that followed weren't funny. I was scared to go back to school. And rightfully so—Hammer Girl later put another girl in the hospital. This time with a combination lock in the girls' locker room.

So I stopped going.

Eventually, the school called my mom. She had never gotten a call like that. I was an inquisitive, if quiet, student. Did the work and did it well. Above all, I'd always shown up.

Trouble? I didn't know her. Not until that moment.

Despite my long absence, the school counselor saw something in me. She told my mother I was a good student, recognizing that my failing grades weren't a reflection of my ability, just the result of too many missed days.

The next thing she said changed everything. There was a program, she explained, that could change everything: Project Advance. It offered a way to make up lost credits and earn college credit at the same time.

Classes would be held at the local community college. Some led by high school teachers, others by actual college professors. But the real appeal? If I tested in, I'd never have to go back to that high school again.

I aced the test.

And just like that, I stepped into a new world. A weirder one. A better one. A pocket of misfit brilliance made up of kids like me—nerdy, quirky, overlooked. Kids who were deeply smart and gloriously strange. A cohort of curious contrarians, budding humanitarians, and thinkers who made the kind of offbeat connections that don't show up on a syllabus.

We were outcasts, but in the best way.

In those two years, I learned what it meant to "find your people." *My tribe.* The joy of shared sensibilities. The comfort of being surrounded by other kids who were still finding themselves—but doing so with open minds and open hearts. We were different in every way you could imagine . . . and somehow still recognized something familiar in one another.

It was the first time I truly understood that community isn't always something you're born into.

Sometimes, it's something you build.

Project Advance was the first of many pivots, all unplanned, reactionary, and necessary. Looking back . . . that moment was the beginning of everything.

Because after the hammer, I didn't just grow up. I fast-forwarded.

PART III

Motherhood, Marriage, and the Great Unraveling

IF THIS CHAPTER HAD A FLAVOR

Baked mac and cheese

IF THIS CHAPTER HAD A SOUNDTRACK

"TO ZION" .... LAURYN HILL

"EX-FACTOR" .... LAURYN HILL

"BUTTERFLY" .... MARIAH CAREY

"THIS WOMAN'S WORK" .... MAXWELL

"GOLDEN" .... JILL SCOTT

By the time most of my peers were in college—drinking, skipping class, and "figuring themselves out"—I was knee-deep in adulting. I had an apartment, a partner, a tech job, and a Costco membership. We weren't married yet, but we were playing house—matching dish towels, long commutes, weekend barbecues. A soft domestic rhythm that felt like proof I was doing adulthood right.

And then came my babies.

I was a young mom. But I could've been an even younger one.

At twenty, I had a miscarriage. So when I got pregnant again at twenty-two, I wasn't scared. I wasn't upset. I was *elated*. Grateful. Ready in the way only someone who's lost and grieved can be.

I was also lucky. I had good insurance. A stable job. A partner who was just as excited as I was.

Pregnancy wasn't easy. I was sick the whole time—relentlessly, humiliatingly sick. I weighed less at nine months pregnant than I had before I got pregnant. I was all belly and anticipation. Bright eyes and zero clues. Including about labor.

I was on the phone with my mom complaining about Braxton Hicks "practice" contractions, when she cut me off mid-sentence: "Mya. You're in labor."

I rolled my eyes. Protested. But eventually, I agreed to go to the hospital.

She lived in San Diego, where the quickest way to get to me was a flight. I'm so glad she knew better than to listen to me, that she decided to hop on that plane.

At the hospital, the nurses monitored the contractions. The doctors kept looking at the ultrasound, taking measurements: the size of my pelvis . . . the size of my son's shoulders. Their faces tightened.

They didn't know if he would fit. They described how this could stall my delivery—or worse.

I chose a C-section.

It was a big decision, especially since I'd planned to give birth naturally—not because I was some earth mama, but because the epidural needle terrified me.

But all that went out the window when they said his shoulder could dislocate.

Everything moved quickly after that. I was prepped for surgery and wheeled into a room where the lights above the table hung lower and burned brighter than the rest of the room—like spotlights on a breakout role I hadn't auditioned for.

I survived the epidural. And in what felt like seconds . . . I could hear the surgical drape rustle, smell the sharp antiseptic, and then—his cry. I was a mom.

My firstborn was carried out of the OR in his father's arms just as my mother arrived. And Candice—the rebel, the mystic, the stoic visionary they called Witchy Poo—*wept*.

Apparently, becoming a grandmother turns you into a crybaby.

She's been more emotional ever since that day.

Tears at commercials.

Tears at birthdays.

Tears just . . . because.

That moment opened her up, and that new, softer *her* has never left.

Everyone saw my baby before I did.

While I was still in recovery, people kept coming into my room saying how beautiful he was.

I was groggy, itchy from the anesthesia, trying to wrestle the fog of a Benadryl injection . . . and more than anything, I just wanted to see him.

Their excitement annoyed me.

*Really? That's great. Wish I could see for my*self.

But when I finally did—it was much more than "love at first sight."

To this day I still can't describe it. But it fueled a behavior people often mistake for "good parenting."

They see the social media posts, the pictures, the constant babble about the baby's milestones and routines and little quirks—and think that's what being a good mom looks like.

What they're witnessing is *obsession.*

I am—and always will be—obsessed.

I couldn't get enough of his little spaghetti lips and his soft brown eyes: always curious, always aware. The way his tiny hand curled around my finger—and like magic, I could tell: From the moment he saw me, he knew I was his mom. My cousin Ferris and I still joke about how I'd slide a mirror under his tiny nose just to make sure he was breathing, because fear and obsession are besties. I named him Journey, after the band (in Candice's house we believed in Steve Perry), and I spent hours daydreaming about all the places he'd go.

I remember that first New Year's Eve after Journey was born. I was twenty-three and his dad was only twenty-seven, so of course he wanted to go out.

As for me?

I was aghast.

He wanted me to leave . . . my baby?

On New Year's Eve?

Absolutely not.

I spent my time breaking every rule I read in parenting books.

I slept with him next to me—out of convenience and concern.

Did you know you can breastfeed and sleep at the same time? I did.

There were so many mornings I woke up to a freed nipple and Journey nestled in the joint of my elbow, sound asleep with his mouth wide open and the tiniest dribble of milk trailing down his chin.

Crib? Unused. Schedule? Just vibes.

And now that I think about it, maybe it wasn't obsession. Maybe it was *addiction*.

Because just fifteen months later, I had a second: Justice.

Journey was born on Bob Marley's birthday. Justice on Malcolm X's. And if you knew them, you'd know how deeply appropriate that is.

Living with Bob and Malcolm—raising these smart, independent, and wildly unpredictable creatures—has been the absolute highlight of my life.

So four years later, when I had Jordan . . . I thought my heart might actually burst.

They say you shouldn't be friends with your kids. But my mom had me at twenty. We grew up together.

I had my boys around the same time in life, and when you grow up together, you become friends. And when you're as addicted as I was (and still am)? You become *best friends.*

I made a lot of mistakes as a parent. Not the headline-worthy kind. Just the quiet, "comes free with purchase when you're parenting while still becoming yourself" kind.

I don't have parenting advice. I have only adoration. I have deeply personal lessons that snuck up on me in the middle of dinner and carpool lines. I have love—wide and deep and stubborn—stretching across the years like memory.

And, of course, I have stories.

When you're raised by a Fort woman, there is no "soft launch" into the facts of life. At five, I asked how babies were made—and I got the full scientific breakdown. No metaphors. No euphemisms. Just biology and clinical clarity.

So years later, when my own five-year-old asked the same question, I gave it to him straight.

He sat with it for a minute, thinking hard. Then, with the horror only a kindergartener can summon, he said, "But her vagina would be so . . . broken."

"You might think so, little man," I said. "But also—like love—it stretches."

And just like that, he carried the knowledge forward.

Weeks later, I overheard him consoling my cousin Ferris. She'd mentioned she was scared to give birth, and without skipping a beat, he said, "Don't worry. Your vagina is stretchy, like a rubber band."

He meant it. With his whole little heart.

He had learned something. And he wanted to share it—to offer comfort.

That's what being a parent has been for me. Not a

performance of perfection, but a lifelong stretch. Of love. Of patience. Of perspective.

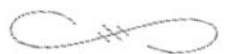

When it came to showing that love, we didn't cut corners. Especially at holiday meals. In my family, mac and cheese was never just food. It was confirmation. We were not a premade, instant dinner kind of family. No foil Velveeta sleeves or powder mixes in sight. You don't get assigned mac and cheese at gatherings unless your dish had proven worthy—and mine had. Bubble at the edges, heavy with history, sacred enough to travel across houses at Thanksgiving. That dish felt like parenting to me: layered with what came before, tweaked with my own hand, carried with reverence. Not performance, but presence. A sacred side dish, a reminder that even when you're tired and carrying everything, you can still bring something divine to the table.

So no, I don't have parenting advice.

But I do have three sons who taught me how to name emotions I once had no words for. Who challenged me to grow in real time. Who made me softer, sharper, and stronger than I ever knew I could be.

And on my thirtieth birthday, with a house already full of boys, I got the opportunity to add one more.

He was five years older than my oldest. Family by DNA—but also something else entirely in spirit.

Technically, he was my younger cousin, a baby of a

twelve-year-old. But he became my son the moment I recognized the need.

Circumstances shifted. Things happened that left him without a safe place to land. And I didn't hesitate.

He came to me and I made room.

It still surprises me how extraordinary people find this part of my story. And I don't mean spectacular or laudable—I mean *extra*-ordinary.

Because honestly?

Who raised me?

My grandmother gave people places to land. My mom, in her small two-bedroom apartment, gave people places to land. *What could be more ordinary?*

This is just what we do.

But motherhood—at least for me—has never been just love.

It's also fear.

Not the everyday kind that pops in for a quick visit when they're sick or running late.

The kind that sits in your chest like a stone—heavy and constant—because you know the world won't always see what you see when they look at your sons.

I don't just love them obsessively. I love them selfishly . . . because they are mine. And I love them selflessly . . . because the world is better with them in it.

But the world?

It doesn't always agree.

The world saw my boys as threats before they were even old enough to understand what that meant. Before they had words for race or bias. Before they could possibly know why I held my breath every single time they walked out the door.

At some point everyone wants their kids to stay little, as long as possible. Some of us have more reasons than others.

I'm only 5'2". But let's just say that my sons began towering over me before they even needed deodorant.

They're now the kind of tall that women prefer on dating profiles. The kind that commands space. Sturdy. Broad. All now over 200 pounds to boot. Beautiful and soft and whole—but you might miss all that at a glance.

Especially with my youngest, Jordan.

In high school, he stood just shy of six feet. Skin rich like cedar. Locks framing his face in a messy, radiant bob. A beautiful gay boy with a rifle in his hand—not for violence, but for art.

You see, he made the rifle line on the color guard team his junior year in high school. And let me tell you, that was a big deal. Years of practice. Late nights. Sore wrists. Pure joy.

Journey and Justice played football, so I knew how to be a football mom. I made custom jerseys, pretended I knew the rules, and cheered like a maniac. Jordan is different—and always was. He didn't want the noise of home crashing into his serene universe of pliés, pirouettes, and sautés. His refined tastes rarely matched the ruckus we as a family are known to bring. But whenever I caught a glimpse of him practicing? *Whew.* It took my breath away. He moved with a strength that disguised itself as grace, translating power into elegance. The performances themselves always served costumes and choreography tied to some story—but for me, they were secondary to the quiet mastery he carried in his body. My baby boy never needed an audience. He just needed space to move the way only he could.

The rifle itself? A painted wooden replica. Functional for exactly nothing except a flip through the air. Brightly colored to exaggerate its harmlessness. A symbol of discipline and artistry and pride.

But when he wanted to take even that bright-white faux rifle outside to practice . . . uncovered, slung over his shoulder?

My heart clenched every time. Because I knew what the world might see.

Not the color guard kid who loves rhythm and precision. Not the discipline in his wrists, the hours of flips and catches that turned wood into art. I knew they might not see any softness at all.

Instead: just a silhouette.

A tall Black boy . . . with something shaped like a gun.

And that's all it takes.

He knows this. I know this. We both carry it now—not as a shared burden, but as a truth we didn't ask for.

I hate that I couldn't protect him from that truth.

That I had to remind him: *Cover it, baby. Hide it. Be careful.*

Because underneath all the pride and practice . . . it's still America out here.

And that rifle? That wooden, painted, beautiful token

of self-expression and high school spirit?

Just another reminder that freedom, for us, always comes with a footnote.

And maybe that's why—even now, in adulthood—I want them near me. I want to put eyes on them. I want to know what they ate for breakfast and whether they made it home.

It's why I call them every day (and, often, not just once). Why our group chats are consistent and incessantly ridiculous. Why the memes and check-ins and "what y'all doing" texts matter.

It's proof of life.

Maybe my obsession isn't just addictive motherly love.

Maybe it's protection.

Maybe it's the only armor I have left to give them—my presence, proximity, prayer. The illusion that if I'm close enough, I can shield them from a world that still hasn't earned the right to witness their brilliance.

So yeah . . . I do want them close.

Because I know what's out there.

And because when they laugh in my kitchen, when they stretch across my couch and eat all my snacks, when they roll their eyes at my questions and still answer anyway—I can exhale.

I knew I wanted to be a mom before I knew I wanted to be a wife. I was definitely better prepared for the former.

I married the man I called my best friend. I was quirky. He was cool. Respected in the streets with just enough bad-boy energy to keep things interesting—but underneath it all, I saw softness. Sensitivity. A gentleness he didn't show the world, but I felt it. And that made me feel safe. Seen. Chosen.

So I did what so many of us do when we want love to last—I tried to become the version of myself I thought he'd love most.

His family was Southern-rooted and full of tradition. The women wore jewelry to breakfast. Matched their purses to their shoes. They knew how to "make a plate" for their man without asking. Femininity was choreography—and I was the new girl trying to learn the steps.

It was a microculture that contrasted everything I'd grown up with. In my family, softness was practical. Femininity wasn't something we performed—it was something we carried. My mom once told me she wanted to be my grandpa's "favorite son," and she meant it. With only three brothers in the mix, she figured the competition was slim, so she set out to outshoot, outfish, and outbuild them all. She looked the part, too. She wore men's cut jeans worn soft at the seams, a cowboy hat tipped just so and, for a while, a man's vest she loved like armor. But even covered in grit, even elbow deep in a busted water heater, she couldn't hide the softness of her frame or the wild curls that fell across her face. My grandpa saw her as a son, yes, but also as a daughter. Both. Always both.

That was the femininity I grew up with. Not an *either/or*,

but a *both/and*. Practical *and* radiant. Tender *and* relentless. Which is why, when I stepped into my in-law's version of femininity, I couldn't help but be intrigued. It felt familiar the way a movie does—recognizable, but not lived. And just foreign enough to feel like *possibility*.

Being around them was like trying on glittery heels you don't need but can't resist. You take them home. Admire them. Convince yourself they'll come in handy. And for a while, they make you feel like someone new. Until one day, years later, you realize . . . they're just not *you*.

They were "traditional" in a way that made Tyler Perry's Madea movies make sense. Unfiltered. Unapologetic. Loud enough to earn side-eyes at my family's dinner table—except that, on them, it was almost musical. Somehow, it worked.

When I stepped into that world, I wasn't trying to pretend. I was experimenting. Softening. Seeing what it felt like to be adored for a version of myself I'd never worn before.

And I liked her.

She was pinker. Softer. Sparkly in a way I didn't hate.

No one asked me to change—but I adapted anyway.

Pinker lip gloss. Quieter laughter. Cookout rituals. Towels folded the "right" way. Jordans traded for clacking sandals. A new kind of womanhood, tried on for size and carried home.

The pinker, sparklier version of me felt gentle. She fit into rooms more easily.

I was still my mother's daughter inside, but on the outside, I had become more palatable.

Then, somewhere along the way . . . I started mistaking adaptability for authenticity. Because when you shapeshift enough times, you start forgetting your original form.

Trimming yourself to fit others can feel like love for a while—until you realize the pieces you cut off were the ones that gave you life.

We looked good on paper. And to most people watching, we made sense. But that pink-and-sparkly version of me started to feel like a mask. One I was holding together with emotional tape that was starting to fail. I had created a version of myself that made him more comfortable. That made his world easier. And the truth is, he didn't ask many questions about who I was becoming underneath all that sparkle. He liked the presentation. The polish. The quiet loyalty. And I—so good at performing stability—kept the act going longer than I should have.

The unraveling didn't come all at once. But it came. Slowly. Over many years. Fifteen, to be exact.

At first, I tried to fit in—professionally, socially, romantically—by shrinking myself. I softened my tone. Wrapped every opinion in a smile. Added disclaimers to my brilliance. Laughed softer. Took up less space. I became easy to like. Easy to praise. Easy to keep around.

And I began to hate it.

Because every time I trimmed myself to fit, I lost something sacred. Something wild. Something that sounded like me.

The girl who grew up in a house where honesty was humor and boldness was love? She started waiting for permission to speak. To feel. To *be*.

That's the thing about trying to be palatable: It starves you slowly. Until one day, you realize you've been hungry for your own voice.

There wasn't one big betrayal. No screaming match. No dramatic exit.

It was much quieter than that.

I loved my husband. I really did. I always saw him as my friend first—someone who would protect me, who knew me, who would never hurt me.

But "never hurt me" is a beautiful idea . . . not a realistic one. Not in any relationship. Not even the good ones.

Still, I believed—deep in my bones—that we were friends. Until I started changing. Expanding. And I noticed the space between us stretching.

Not because of something unforgivable. Just . . . moments.

Like how dancing in public embarrassed him. How my sense of play made him uncomfortable. How my idea of marriage—as two whole people orbiting together instead of one fused planet—felt to him like chaos.

To me, it was freedom. To him, it was a threat.

And that's when I started wondering, *Does he even* like *me? Do* I *like* him*?*

Because love without like is polite. It's functional. Maybe it means well. But it can't hold you.

And I wanted to be held.

The end came slowly. In the quiet. While folding laundry. Driving in silence. Pausing before answering the question, "What's wrong?" Because the truth didn't fit into small talk.

There was no single moment. Just a growing ache. The sense that I was living next to someone—not *with* them. And more than that . . . next to *him*, I was shrinking.

The more I came back to myself, the less room there was for me in that life.

It took years to admit. Even longer to say out loud: *This isn't what love is supposed to feel like. This isn't what partnership should cost.*

The moment I knew we were done didn't come with a scream. It came with a silence. A bone-deep exhaustion from translating myself. From dimming. From carrying a version of life that didn't have air for the woman I was becoming.

I had been the version of me that fit *his* world. Now I wanted the version of me that fit mine.

So I let it go.

And I wish I could tell you that life approved. That it gave me a gold star and a launching pad. That the next chapter opened with ease and welcoming applause.

Nope.

To understand what came next, we have to go back—about six years before the divorce.

We were young, the kind of young that made it easy for us to pass as college kids sneaking into happy hour. Me with my too-big hoop earrings and him with that grin that encouraged trouble. Our roles weren't traditional. I worked in tech sales, carrying the paycheck, while he stayed home with the boys. For me, it affirmed what I had always known myself to be: provider and nurturer. I leaned into him as a protector. But that role never sat easily on his shoulders. He became both husband and dependent, gambling away savings in a string of sports debts.

To recover, we moved to Georgia. For me, it was a return. For us, a new beginning. And we thrived.

It was the kind of suburban life you see in TV shows, the yellow bus wheezing to a stop right in front of our driveway, kids tumbling out with backpacks bigger than their bodies. Neighbors waved from across manicured lawns and actually knew our boys' names. Saturdays meant yard sales and lemonade stands. Fourth of July meant block parties where paper plates bent under the weight of ribs, and the one nosy neighbor proudly unveiled something called "Snickers salad." I remember staring at that bowl like it had broken all the rules. Candy bars and Cool Whip pretending to be produce? Nope. Not a salad I grew up with, but apparently a new Southern delicacy.

For five years, that was our life. Cookouts and cul-de-sacs. Familiar faces at the grocery store. A house that felt steady. It was the closest thing to the dream I'd ever known.

And then, the dream cracked.

Slowly at first, then suddenly. As sudden as a phone call beginning with, "We're restructuring," and ending with, "We'll need your laptop by Friday."

To be fair, the severance was generous. And at first, I treated it like a gift. A pause. A clean break.

I told myself I needed rest. That I'd use the time to figure out what I really wanted next.

But the truth is—I didn't rest. I redirected.

I threw myself into building a bakery from scratch. Woke up earlier, worked longer, poured every ounce of energy into dough and hope. The ovens smelled like promise, but the register told another story. Passion doesn't always equal profit, and flour doesn't pay the mortgage. I made less money than I'd ever seen as an adult. So much less that I couldn't afford the life I had built.

And still—I kept pretending I was okay. Smiled through networking events. I talked about "new chapters" like I wasn't aching. Avoided driving past the sprawling campuses where I once worked. Took long detours just to keep from seeing them. Told myself it didn't matter. That I was fine.

But the layoff was more than a career shift. It ended, with a single perfunctory phone call, ten years of work. A whole era of my life. Beyond just a job, it was a part of my identity. When they let me go, it felt like a breakup. And I never fully grieved it.

In the end, all that dough and hope couldn't save us. The layoff meant uprooting my entire family and moving across the country. And I felt like a failure, a feeling both unfamiliar and intolerable to me, especially at that time.

I had to get back to a job that paid the bills. I found one: in California.

At first, we stayed with his mother while I started a new job and searched for a place of our own. It was temporary, a holding pattern until we found our footing. But that house made something clear to me that I had not yet admitted: I could not find home in him.

That part was not sudden. It was the culmination of a million little moments. The big betrayals like gambling and infidelity were easier to forgive. Those came with drama and apologies, cycles I understood. What broke me were the whispers, the quiet signals that my truest self was not wanted in the marriage. That kind of rejection does not explode. It erodes.

So when I finally signed the lease, I knew he would not be moving in. That was the real beginning of the divorce, not a lawyer's letterhead or stamped paperwork, but a set of keys that no longer fit his hand. This was not some dramatic failure with flames or noisy collapse, but the slow, quiet kind that seeps into your bones. Until then, I had never really failed. I had been the good student, the one who always nailed the interview, the one who followed the rules and was rewarded.

But this time? The layoff? The bakery falling short of what I'd dreamed? The divorce that followed?

It wasn't just one failure. It was all of them. Multiplied.

Losing the title of "wife"? That I could imagine. That was manageable.

For about a year we negotiated a new normal. Custody schedules. Football games. School drop-offs. Me not keeping a promise to not date until the divorce was final. It was messy and strange, but I told myself *we* were making it through.

What came next . . . not so much.

The lump was small. At first, I thought I imagined it. No family history. No red flags. Just a whisper from my body that said, "Check again."

And when I did, the knowing dropped in before the doctor ever said a word.

Breast cancer.

The words hung in the air like smoke. Thick. Heavy. Unreal. I could barely hear the treatment plan over the static in my mind.

Everything else—life, plans, feelings—all blurred.

Suddenly, everything revolved around survival. Appointments. Tests. Decisions. Words like *oncologist*, *mastectomy*, and *reconstruction* entered my daily vocabulary. My body stopped feeling like home and started feeling like a project. A battlefield or blueprint. Something to navigate and negotiate with daily.

Whatever strength I thought I had left . . . well, it had to stretch even further.

I tried to power through gracefully.

I showed up with lip gloss and a smile. I joked with the nurses. I reassured everyone I was fine.

But I wasn't.

Not even close.

I was tired in a way that sleep couldn't fix. Lonely in a way that company couldn't cure. And I couldn't pretend anymore.

That's when the breakdown came.

Not in a hospital. Not at a support group. But in my bedroom. Alone. I was separated but not yet divorced, although the process was underway. I had just gotten off the phone with my not-quite-ex-husband to tell him about the surgery—about the cancer. To confirm he'd have the kids while I had to stay in the hospital.

He said, "Sorry to hear that," and then,

"I have a daughter now. She was born today. I'm taking the boys to see her."

I didn't know he had a baby on the way.

Did he just say he was taking the boys to meet her? Our boys?

My mind skipped past him and landed on them.

I didn't even know he was dating. *We* didn't know he was dating, so this baby felt like a plot twist no one saw coming. This, from the same man who, not long ago, had asked me to stay single until the divorce was final.

Our sons were still young—eight, twelve, and thirteen—with quiet hopes of reconciliation tucked between video games and late-night whispers. I knew this would shake them.

As for me, I was too stunned to form anything real. What slipped out was flat and flimsy: a hollow congratulations followed by the only request I could muster. *Let me know how the boys take it.*

I immediately drove to my sister's house and told

her. She looked at me aghast and said, "How are you not crying?"

And the truth was, I didn't know.

Maybe I had cried all I could in invisible ways. Maybe my nervous system was out of words and feelings. Maybe holding it all together had become such a part of me that I'd forgotten how to fall apart.

Until I did.

That night, I sat on the edge of the bed and finally let myself feel.

I cried until I couldn't breathe. I cried for the job I lost. For the marriage I left. For the body that betrayed me. For the baby—my own sons' sister—I hadn't even known was coming. For the ways I kept putting parts of myself down just to be loved. For the woman I used to be—and the one I was still trying to find.

And somewhere between the sobs and the stillness . . . something shifted.

I felt something akin to peace.

Not relief. Not resolution. Just a growing, restful *let it be.* A quiet breath that oxygenated my entire body. A reminder that I was still here. Still whole. The days after that didn't get magically easier. Healing isn't linear. But something had shifted.

I had stopped pretending I was okay. I had stopped trying to "earn" my rest.

For the first time in my adult life, I let people take care of me. Without apology. Without performance.

And somewhere into the mix . . . in came Drew.

Soft-footed. Steady. Right on time.

Technically, he was a not-so-successful Tinder hookup. My first tentative foray into dating post-separation. We met with different intentions—but somehow, they led us to exactly the right place.

The chemistry wasn't *quite* there romantically. But the connection? Instant. We became best friends before either of us could name it.

He showed up in my life at a time when I was unmoored. A little raw. A little scared. And completely in need of someone who didn't require me to explain myself.

He was that person.

The one who texted back. Who showed up with snacks and sarcasm. Who sat with my silence and didn't rush to fix it.

He was the first person who saw me clearly in that strange, in-between season. The first person who didn't need me to be either the woman I had been or the one I was becoming.

Just me. And—this still amazes me—*him*. Because when I thought I felt a lump, he was the one who confirmed I wasn't imagining it.

Intimate. A little awkward. But somehow, cosmically appropriate.

Because Drew has always seen what others miss. Like he's known me for lifetimes.

Even though our friendship was less than a year old when I was diagnosed, when he came to my rescue—it didn't feel strange. It felt like something the universe had prescheduled.

He called to check on me, and I said I was fine. I wasn't, and he knew it. But he didn't push. Didn't ask questions I wasn't ready to answer. Didn't try to rescue me with words.

He just came over. Laid next to me. Let the silence be enough.

He stayed. And then he left.

No big moment. No follow-up. No asking for credit.

It has been eleven years, and Drew is still one of my favorite people. In many ways, he was the first to meet the version of me who was returning to myself. He had fresh eyes because he hadn't known me before, and in some ways he knew me better than people who had known me for decades. He didn't carry old stories or expectations, so he saw me as I was. And he let me lean on him as protector, a role I have never been good at managing for myself.

That's what real care looks like. It's not loud. It's not poetic. It doesn't demand explanation or payback. It just holds space and keeps holding it—even when you don't know what to say.

I used to think love had to be earned. That rest had to be justified. That falling apart made you less worthy of being chosen.

But in that season—when I had nothing shiny to offer—I learned the opposite.

The people who stayed didn't need me to be polished,

let alone pink and sparkly. They also didn't need me to perform my pain. They just showed up.

That's what saved me.

Not the answers. Not the advice.

The presence.

And now?

I don't measure love by how loudly it shows up. I measure it by how gently it stays.

Meals appeared on my doorstep. Someone picked up my prescriptions. Tanesha washed my hair over a sink while we talked about nothing and everything. I didn't resist it—not this time.

I had finally stopped translating my needs into neat little packages.

I just . . . let people show up, or not.

And they did.

Not just my friends. My cousins. My aunts. My mama. People I didn't even realize had been watching. Had been waiting. Had been ready.

That's when I learned the real definition of family. It's not just who you start out with or grow up with. It's who keeps showing up when everything's ugly.

And it turns out, family can take forms you don't expect.

After the divorce, even after the surprise baby girl and all the contradictory feelings that kicked up, my ex and I started a tradition: Sunday dinner.

With my very Fort upbringing and the way my parents co-parented, I just assumed that once I filed for divorce, we'd slide right back into best friend territory. In my head there were double dates, game nights, maybe even vacations together, where everybody got along. Sunday dinners felt like a natural next step for me. For my ex-husband, it took a little longer to get there. I'm pretty sure he thought I lost my mind entirely.

It certainly wasn't about rekindling romance. That had long left the building. It was about continuity. About showing the kids—our shared community—that we were still family. That even when the form changes, the love doesn't have to.

He'd bring something from the grill. I'd make greens, yams, and mac and cheese. Always, mac and cheese. We'd sit, talk, laugh—or sometimes barely speak. And honestly? It was awkward as hell at first.

But it was also kind. Quietly generous.

That tradition didn't last forever. It didn't need to.

Because it was never about the food. It was about presence. The showing up. The ritual of *I'm still here.*

That's what I've come to believe family is. Not the perfection of structure, but the consistency of love. The truth that some people only know how to love you when you're easy . . . and others show up when you're laid bare.

And sometimes, love shows up in forms you never imagined.

Like falling in love with your ex-husband's (*not your*) baby—while you're still technically married.

Like saying *yes*, without flinching, when the infant's mother asks if you'd take care of her if the unthinkable ever happened.

I didn't hesitate. Didn't need time to process.

Because love—real love—isn't about possession. It's not about holding tight to what was. It's about honoring what is. About showing up where love is still needed, even when the story no longer centers you.

I didn't say *yes* because I was over it. I said *yes* because I had evolved past the version of myself that needed things to look a certain way in order to feel valid.

The baby, *our* baby, the little human who taught my sons tenderness, was perfection. The new family, in its own messy way, was still connected to mine.

And that moment—being asked, being trusted, being included—reminded me: You can lose everything you thought mattered . . . and still have love waiting for you on the other side.

Not the old love. Not the predictable kind.

But the love you make space for once you've burned the script.

There is no "lesson learned" onstage bow at the end of grief. There's just the practice of becoming. The choice, every day, to listen a little closer. To soften a little more. To show up even when you don't have all the answers.

To say *yes* to a love that's bigger than loss.

PART IV
Narrative Is Inheritance

IF THIS CHAPTER HAD A FLAVOR

Key lime pie

IF THIS CHAPTER HAD A SOUNDTRACK

"FAMILY REUNION" .... THE O'JAYS

"DANCE WITH MY FATHER" .... LUTHER VANDROSS

"PAPA WAS A ROLLING STONE" .... THE TEMPTATIONS

"JUST MY IMAGINATION" .... THE TEMPTATIONS

"AND THE BEAT GOES ON" .... THE WHISPERS

I was raised by women, but I was shaped by my father. Through legend and DNA. Through whispers over dinner and a grin I inherited without instruction.

I'm proud of the relationship I have with him now. He's seventy-one—not an old seventy-one, if you ask him (and he'd want you to know that). I'd agree. He's sharp. Witty. The kind of man who slips wisdom into a joke and doesn't wait around to see if you catch it.

My dad is a man of ritual. Never jeans. Always slacks,

neatly pressed. Always a fork and knife, even with chicken legs. And, if it's on the menu, *always* key lime pie. Sweet and sharp at once, just like him. Predictable in the best way, a slice of certainty in a world full of contradictions. That pie became shorthand for my father. Polished but with bite, ordinary but spiked with story. A constant I could count on, even when other parts of him were harder to hold.

And that's what surprised me.

Boomers—bless them—aren't always known for their emotional transparency. So when he asked me a feelings-based question, it stopped me. Not in a bad way. In the kind of way that lets you know someone's been carrying something in their spirit long enough to want release.

"How did my absence affect you when you were growing up?"

It's the kind of question that ripples. The kind that echoes through all the rooms you've ever been a child in.

Even though my reflex was to say, "It didn't," I knew that wasn't true. Or at least . . . not the whole truth.

So I sat with it.

And I wrote him this letter instead:

Dear Daddy,

You asked me how I felt about our relationship growing up and how it affected me. And honestly? That's a big, layered question—one that probably deserves a bigger, layered answer.

I think on some level, daddy issues are a universal truth. Every child is shaped by the presence or absence of their father, by what is given and what is withheld. But I didn't grow up feeling like I was missing something. I was left in the hands of a community, wrapped in the arms of Amazonian women and men who raised me as their own. I was called daughter, niece, granddaughter by people who made sure I never felt untethered. And yet, even in your absence, you were present. Your name carried warmth in our home, tucked into stories told over dinner, in the way people sang your praises anytime a Whispers song played.

Grandpa had that quintessential dad energy—stoic, sarcastic, smelling like Texas (which, in his case, was a mix of Vantage 300 cigarettes and Smirnoff screwdrivers, sometimes leading to a sideways walk to bed). He existed in a sea of women, his three sons nearly swallowed up by the force of his eight daughters, and yet his presence never got lost. I admired him, the role he played, the balance of strength and tenderness he carried. And he, too, spoke highly of you.

So, in many ways, I knew you before I ever really knew you. I believed in the idea of you, the way I believed my family when they told me I was a good girl. It wasn't until I got older that I started to see the contrast—the man I was told you were and the man who sometimes failed to show up.

Here's what I think is important: I never doubted that you loved me. Even when you weren't there, your love made its way to me in the stories my mother told, in the times she smoothed over my heartbreak and filled in the gaps with reminders of who you were. She defended you, not out of guilt or regret, but because she believed in your goodness. And because of that, so did I.

When life kicked me in the face at nineteen, I got the chance to really know you. And what a gift that was. To sit across from you and see myself reflected back—not just in our shared features, but in our humor, our mannerisms, our way of looking at the world. Turns out, some relationships only need DNA to mature. And I feel lucky, so lucky, that I got to know you at an age when I could truly appreciate you—not just as my father, but as a person.

So yes, being raised by a fortress of women shaped me. Maybe I would have turned out a little differently if you had been more present when I was growing up. But here's the thing—I love who I am. And I love you, too.

And maybe love, like time, isn't linear. Maybe it loops and bends, finding its way to where it's meant to be, even if the path is unexpected. So, if you ever wonder whether I wish things had been different, know this: I don't need to rewrite history. I just need you to know that I see you, I appreciate you, and I'm grateful for what we have.

Always,
Your daughter

My mom met my father backstage at the Oakland Coliseum. He played lead guitar for a popular R&B group, The Whispers.

A church girl she was not—more modest rebel than groupie. Purposefully meddlesome, oddly a rule follower, and allergic to anything that felt like performance. She stood just outside the dressing room door, arms likely crossed, firmly planted in her principles.

The dressing room, she argued, implied a level of intimacy she wasn't about to entertain. Her sister and cousin didn't share the same hesitation, so they disappeared inside. But she waited. Leaned on the wall like a woman with her own gravitational pull.

And fate—or timing, or mild social claustrophobia—brought my father to that same hallway. He stepped out and found her there.

That hallway birthed a romance. Not one that lasted a lifetime. But one that lasted long enough to create me . . . and to leave an impression on my mother's side of the family that still lingers.

My dad spent a lot of time on the road. By the time I was two, my parents had divorced. I have no memory of their relationship. What I do remember are the periodic visits. A drop-in at my grandmother's house. A few spring breaks. The occasional summer.

When I talk about my parents as a pair, I describe them as "a little bit hippie and a little bit rock and roll."

But if we're being real? My mom is the barefoot rebel with the brass heart. And my dad . . . well, he's way more buttoned-up than your average rocker.

He might have toured the world, but to this day, I have never seen my father in a pair of jeans.

Because my dad was a musician, whenever a song from the group he played with came on the radio, someone—an aunt, a cousin, a neighbor with good taste—would shout, "Turn it up! Mya, that's your daddy!"

And I'd swell. With pride. With story. With the kind of belonging you don't have to explain.

A story almost always followed. Sometimes sweet. Sometimes chaotic. Sometimes halfway true. But it didn't matter.

Because at that moment, he was legend.

And I was his daughter.

Eventually, my dad moved to Georgia. And at nineteen, I showed up on his doorstep.

I had flunked out of college—brilliant but untethered, more familiar with crashing waves than midterms. By the time I landed at his house, I didn't want independence—I wanted a refrigerator I didn't have to restock and a break from pretending I had it all together. I would've followed just about any rule in exchange for room and board.

And rules? Oh, there were many.

Curfew: 9 p.m.

Church: twice a week.

Tone: soft, respectful, no sarcasm. (Which meant: no *me.*)

I was my mom's only baby by birth. But on my father's side, I was the youngest—and probably his most problematic. There, I was one of five, with two sisters and two brothers, a mix of step and half that made family feel more like a blend than a straight line.

His office employed his three daughters. It was the headquarters of a man building something bigger, and everyone brought their quirks to the work—but mine was always the same. My gift was protest.

My power was loopholes.

My love language? Boundary testing.

For a man who'd never deign to wear jeans . . . image matters.

And for a Black entrepreneur in Georgia, it's more than appearance—it's survival. My dad demanded professionalism. Crisp lines. Clear expectations. No exceptions. And when he asked me to wear stockings to work, I refused.

That was the first time I got fired.

Not because I was bad at the job—because I was bad at following his version of the rules. And his rules weren't arbitrary. They were armor.

He knew what the world required of a Black business owner in the South, and he was trying to teach me how to move with that understanding.

This is the same man who created an entire faux *white boss* alter ego—same voice, different name. Let's pause to give this alter ego some shine, because it was genius. Over the phone, my dad's voice carried a kind of racial ambiguity. As the owner of a staffing agency that also operated government contracts, a lot of his business started with phone calls. But when people finally met him in person, they were often surprised or even unsettled to realize he was a Black man. In the South, depending on the prospect, that revelation could be a deal-breaker. Other times, they simply assumed he could not possibly be the owner and would ask to be referred to the boss.

That is how "John Tomlin" was born. A fictitious white man, worn over the phone by my father whenever he needed a white man to vouch for his work.

He knew how to navigate that world. And he tried to pass that wisdom down in rules, routines, resourcefulness, and starch.

But I was nineteen. Full of Fort-girl fire and pierced rebellion. I understood myself—just not yet the system. And I wasn't ready to learn it on his terms.

Still, no hard feelings.

And then . . . I came back.

By the time I returned to his office, I had discovered instant messaging. This was the late 1900s—a golden era of digital rebellion.

My desk had a view of the walkway my dad used when returning from the field. So I became the lookout.

"Cuckoo! Cuckoo!" I'd call out like a cartoon parrot.

And with that single warning, every browser window closed. Every message thread disappeared. Every daughter in the building went silent.

We weren't supposed to be using IM. So we pretended not to.

It worked. Until it didn't. Eventually, we got caught.

We all got fired.

And then . . . we went to the mall. Dismissed, but not devastated.

I learned a few things that day. That it's easy to stand on principle when your rent's not on the line. I had a place to stay. My stakes were soft. Conviction came cheap.

I also learned that being good at your job doesn't make you exempt from the rules. I turned those Yellow Page leads into paying clients. I was bringing in business.

And I still got fired.

Because for my dad, it wasn't just about talent. It was about trust.

About tone.

About how we carry ourselves inside someone else's scrutiny.

And this was the late 1900s, y'all. Before hashtags. Before Slack. Before "just hopping on Zoom." We were rogue agents with AOL Instant Messenger, winging it in pencil skirts and too much eyeliner.

And my father—the man with a faux *white boss* alter ego and an ironed crease sharp enough to split atoms—was not having it.

Still, through all that? He kept showing up.

And so did I.

The bond we formed in those messy in-between years has never cracked.

Eventually, I left Georgia. Moved back to California. Chased the tech dream.

Got grown. Got humbled. Got better.

And here's the twist:

The tech dream?

It started as a sales job.

Turns out, being handed a Yellow Pages book and turning it into a pipeline of real customers is excellent training for becoming a sales rep in tech. *Who knew?*

All those hours cold-calling strangers . . . All that rejection, all that improv, all that "Hi, do you have a moment to talk?" hustle—

It translated.

The job my dad fired me from?

It quietly became the foundation for the career that changed my life.

Years later, I came back to Georgia—not as the rebellious daughter with a suitcase and soft consequences . . . but as a mother, a wife, and a woman with her own house, her own babies, her own version of "grown."

Dad and I were different now. Older. Softer, maybe. Or just clearer.

I was a provider now—understanding consequence and sacrifice through a lens I was once too young to see. The rules that once felt rigid now read like protection. The starch. The standards. The sharp creases in his pants. I didn't just recognize them anymore; I also related.

He had found a deeper spiritual identity by then—Jewish. Faithful in a way that might've confused other people. But not me.

Because when you're raised with gospel on Sundays, incense on Tuesdays, and Taoist texts in the bathroom—belief becomes less about who's "right" and more about what holds. What carries you through. What cracks you open and makes you feel loved.

My whole life, the people I've loved have followed different paths. When that's your reality, you learn to stop needing things to match. You start paying attention to the common thread—love, discipline, ritual, reverence. You see the sacred in the overlap. You start recognizing God . . . everywhere.

So no, I wasn't surprised by my father's new rituals. I was comforted.

And the gift?

He gave that to my children, too.

They were six and seven the first time they visited the synagogue. Wide-eyed. Slightly confused. And completely unbothered by the difference. They called it "the synagarten"—which made me laugh out loud and tear up all at once. Because to them, it was storytime and bagels. A quiet room where people spoke in soft tones and shared something holy.

They didn't know the prayers by heart. They didn't need to.

Because what they felt . . . was inclusion. Rhythm. Peace.

And I watched, quietly, as my father's faith became another thread in the tapestry we were building—one that held gospel and Hebrew, science and spirit, rebellion and ritual.

Years later, those same kids—now also grown—still carry that memory. They've seen faith in many robes. They've tasted God in communion wafers and challah bread. And they've had to endure Luther Vandross in grainy VHS with Mama Nita . . . which, let's be honest, is its own kind of religion.

So when my ex-husband once told them, "Your mom doesn't believe in God," I didn't argue.

I get it.

Because when you tell your husband—who was raised Pentecostal, with traditional values and a deep reverence for church shoes and choir protocol—that you and your mother have, on more than one occasion, attempted to make voodoo dolls . . . when your sense of humor includes the occasional baby Jesus joke . . . and when you describe yourself as "spiritual" instead of religious?

That spells "godless." To him, anyway.

Rather than telling, I just kept showing them what I believe.

Because I don't need a steeple to find the sacred.

God is in everything—if you know how to look.

If there's a theme running through these memories—these firings, fabrications, father-daughter friction—it's this:

Narrative is inheritance.

Not just the stories we're told, but the way we internalize them. The tone in which they're delivered. The parts they skip. The parts we cling to.

My family—especially the women—never let my father become a villain in the story. Even in his absence, his presence was offered to me with softness. With reverence. With just enough myth to keep me proud and just enough fact to keep me grounded.

That shaped me.

It shaped the way I spoke about my sons' father. It shaped the way I held space for both his flaws and his effort. It shaped the way I made room for complexity—not just in others, but in myself.

There is something divine about refusing to shrink a whole person down to the parts they couldn't give you. My father was on the road with his band while I was curled up on my grandmother's sofa. I never carried a sad stigma about him, because the women in my life refused to let me. They wove him into my story even when he wasn't in the room. They made sure I had someone to take me to the father-daughter dances, someone to stand in the gap.

When you believe your dad is T'Challa, you're willing to make concessions for Black Panther. So when The Whispers came on the radio, I didn't ache. I turned it up. I let the rhythm and blues settle into my skin and pores with pride. With recognition.

My dad.

There's a kind of love that shows up as protection of reputation. That's what my family did for me. It's what I've tried to do for my boys. When I say I was raised by women, I mean I was raised by editors of memory—people who knew how to frame absence without bitterness. People who knew that sometimes, protecting the story is how you protect the child.

Now, as an adult, I can hold the whole picture:

My dad was imperfect. He also taught me resilience, structure, and grace. He fired me twice and still took my calls. He wore a perfectly ironed shirt to every occasion and never once wore jeans. He found a faith that steadied him. And when he asked me how his absence shaped me—it wasn't to fix the past. It was to hold space for the truth of it.

That, too, is love. And that's the story I carry.

PART V

The Messy In-Between

IF THIS CHAPTER HAD A FLAVOR

Spicy shrimp tacos

IF THIS CHAPTER HAD A SOUNDTRACK

"WHAT YOU WON'T DO FOR LOVE"	BOBBY CALDWELL
"WICKED GAMES"	THE WEEKND
"I LIKE THAT"	JANELLE MONAE
"6 INCH"	BEYONCÉ
"GOOD DAYS"	SZA

Breast cancer ended up being the best thing that ever happened to me.

Before I go any further, I need to say this out loud: This is by no means a universal truth.

For too many, breast cancer does not represent a beginning, only an ending. A diagnosis that leads not to healing, but to heartbreak. To timelines cut short. To bodies betrayed. To goodbyes no one was ready to say. I want to name them.

The women—and the men—who didn't get to finish their stories.

Whose laughter lives in memories.

Whose birthdays are honored with candles, photos, and the sharp ache of absence. I speak this next part in their shadow.

In their honor. Because for me—and I can speak only for me—cancer didn't take everything. It gave me something I didn't know I was allowed to have.

It undid me in a way that made space for truth. Not in a poetic way.

In the kind of way that leaves you blinking at your life, whispering,

How did I get here?

What now? At first, there was the leave from work. Four months.

I probably only needed one.

But I took the others.

To breathe.

To reset.

To reintroduce myself . . . to myself. Cancer gave me permission to stop performing.

To stop being the "strong one." The helpful one. The functioning-through-it-all one.

And with that permission came clarity—the kind that only arrives in stillness. It also gave me a body I didn't know I wanted. I had a mastectomy.

The time between pre-diagnosis and treatment was the most excruciating part. I wasn't new to breast lumps. I'd had atypical cells removed before and thought I knew the routine. But this time the doctors moved with an urgency I'd never seen. A mammogram, ultrasound, and biopsy all in one day. Two days later, while at work, the call came. I scribbled words I barely understood:

Pleomorphic. HER2 positive. Cancer. Fuck.

At thirty-five, I had cancer.

What I felt was more than fear. It was a primal urge to get as far away from the diagnosis as I could. I wanted to run away, and with Thanksgiving as an excuse, the boys and I went to Arizona. We packed up the car and hit the road together. After what felt like forever on the highway, I pulled up to Miesha's house. Miesha is Auntie Red's daughter, four years my senior.

We grew up side by side because our moms were inseparable, which meant I was always in her atmosphere, whether she liked it or not. She wasn't allowed to do much without me in tow. Dates? Guess who tagged along? Me! Happily. *Annoyingly.* The way only a little cousin can relish. She was my preview of things to come. My blueprint for adolescence.

In true Miesha fashion, when I arrived, she greeted me exactly as expected: impossibly happy and incredibly excited. Miesha loves a Walmart run almost as much as she loves my cooking. Even though I was exhausted from a twelve-hour drive and still reeling from *FUCKING CANCER*, she insisted I go with her. She sang in the store, unbothered by my grouchiness. And I, in return, wanted to strangle that angelic voice right out of her. Every way I had once delighted in annoying her growing up had been flipped back on me, with interest. I was annoyed but entirely grateful, because in the moment, contemplating Miesha's untimely demise was much better than being consumed by cancer.

We cooked, and the house felt like a harbor. Surgery came in December. The mass was removed and pathology confirmed malignancy. Noninvasive for now, but sneaky, the kind that likes to show up where you don't expect it.

Those weeks turned me into a reluctant scholar of medical papers. I learned the language of survival, leaned on my people, and watched my sons be steadier than I had any right to expect. With a 40–60 percent chance of recurrence, I made the choice that would allow me to be here for them.

I decided to have a double mastectomy. It felt brutal to say it out loud and merciful to have an end in sight.

My treatment was all surgery. No chemo. No radiation. And I *just said no* to hormone therapy. Years earlier, I had undergone an emergency hysterectomy that coincided with the birth of my third child. So when cancer came, choosing surgery felt less like a decision and more like a pattern. Before the double mastectomy, I wondered what this meant for my womanhood. Without breasts, without a uterus, did I still qualify? In retrospect, the concern feels trivial compared to the alternative. But at the moment, it was all consuming.

Reconstruction was covered by insurance.

I chose what's called a "DIEP flap"—fat from my belly, moved to my chest. Translation?

Flat stomach.

New breasts.

Zero guilt about the glow-up. I couldn't wait to take it for a spin.

Welcome to the messy in-between. I was thirty-five, but in many ways, I was living my twenties for the first time. In my actual twenties, I didn't drink. Didn't club. Didn't explore.

Not because I wasn't curious—

But because my husband wasn't comfortable with any of it.

I was trying to be the version of me that felt . . . acceptable. Which is funny, in hindsight.

Because he loved a drink—Hennessy, neat, always.

Loved his weed, too. Rolled it tight, smoked it slow.

But me?

I was the sober, steady one.

The designated driver. The one making sure the vibes didn't go left. Because I thought being "good" meant being tame. And being tame meant being chosen.

He'd placed me on a pedestal I never asked to stand on. And when I stepped down, I realized how much I had missed.

So when the marriage ended and the body was rebuilt, I gave myself permission to find out what I liked. Turns out?

I liked a lot. And when it came to men, some liked me back. One, even enough to gift an "engagement pebble."

But first, another: a rapper-entrepreneur and former pimp, who somehow made all the wrong things feel wildly right—for a moment. What they had in common was this:

They both met the real me.

No representative. No curated first-date version.

Just me. Because after the marriage, I made a promise: No one would fall in love with my performance again. I led with my whole self.

And that kind of openness?

It's disarming. They thought they were getting a preview.

I gave them the full person.

Soft, layered, honest. Not because I was desperate.

Because I was done playing small. And with that version of me came a different kind of magnetism. The kind that pulled in unexpected people. Men I never would've noticed before—and men who never would've known what to do with the old me. One of them caught me completely off guard.

The kind of man you don't plan to meet.

The kind you definitely don't plan to enjoy. But there he was. And truthfully?

I was an enigma to him. For someone who had managed women professionally, he couldn't quite wrap his head around a woman who didn't have an angle. Who wasn't trying to use him, fix him, or be chosen by him. Who offered help without keeping score. Who was curious—not about what he had, but who he was. He had stories.

Whew, he had stories. I should've known he wasn't normal when he introduced himself with a nickname I won't print here and a grin that made you forget to ask questions. He smelled like cologne and bad ideas.

First, I found out he was a rapper.

Then an entrepreneur.

Then—a retired pimp. I thought he was joking. He wasn't. Somewhere between the shrimp tacos and the way he rolled a blunt with a surgeon's precision . . .

I realized I was being seen. Not because he wanted something.

But because—for once—someone didn't. He didn't flinch at my depth.

Didn't ask me to shrink.

Didn't try to box me in or back me into a definition. He let me be. And for a brief moment, that was enough. But he didn't just leave me with stories.

He was my gateway drug. Quite literally. I tried edibles for the first time because of him. He had a cannabis business—fully licensed, surprisingly organized, and, dare I say . . . legit.

He offered me one. Just one.

I took it like a rookie.

No questions. No pacing. No idea what I was in for. About forty-five minutes later . . . I was melting. At light speed. And in slow motion. My legs heavy, my mouth cotton-dry, laughter echoing off the walls like it had its own reverb.

I laughed so hard I cried.

Then cried so hard I forgot why I was laughing.

And in the middle of that dizzy, disorienting high—between the floating and the surrender—I felt something else: Safe. Not because I was in control.

But because, for once, I wasn't trying to be. That edible didn't make me wild.

It reminded me I was alive. And for a moment . . . I got to be the "bad girl."

The one who didn't ask permission.

Who said yes for no reason at all.

Who danced on tables and flirted in low lighting and disappeared when she felt like it.

The one who didn't explain herself.

And then there was another—the one who came in softer but fell hard.

He was young. And honestly, they all were. There was something about a twenty-something energy that matched where I was in life.

Both of us figuring things out.

Both of us exploring adulthood for the first time—me, post-marriage and reborn . . . and him, just stepping into his own skin.

He was beautiful.

Open to love without restriction.

The kind of soft-hearted that still believed in *forever*, even if he didn't say it out loud.

And me? I was open too.

But in a way that protected my freedom like oxygen.

He freed my body, softened something in me I hadn't touched in years. He got my dark humor, met it with tenderness. And the sex?

Whew.

Let's just say he reminded me I had a body worth

worshipping.

He wanted all of me.

I just wanted to experience him. Not possess him. Not keep him.

Just . . . feel him.

And that became the disconnect. Not because I wasn't honest.

But because the intimacy I gave—so casually, so completely—felt like a promise I never made. And I broke his heart not with betrayal, but with clarity.

Right before a work trip to the Philippines, he gave me a box.

A small gift to open mid-flight.

He also gave me instructions: "First, watch *The Pebble and the Penguin*. Then open it."

So I did.

The Pebble and the Penguin is a sweet animated film about a shy penguin named Hubie who falls in love and goes on a dangerous, ridiculous journey just to bring the perfect pebble to the penguin he adores.

He risks everything for that gesture.

All for the chance to be chosen.

I sat there, thirty thousand feet in the air, eating warm nuts in business class and dreading what was in the damn box.

After the movie, I opened it.

Inside was a smooth, flat stone.

A literal pebble.

I laughed.

Then paused.

Then sat with the quiet thud of "oh no."

Because I knew.

When I returned from that trip, I had been planning to have a conversation. I needed more space.

More truth.

More freedom than my patience could stretch around.

But before I could even unpack my bag, he met me at the airport . . . holding a life-sized teddy bear.

I'd just stepped off a fifteen-hour flight. Hair in a bun. Hoodie on. Not a lick of emotional energy to spare.

And there he was.

Smiling. Hopeful. Still carrying that pebble in his heart.

And all I could think to say was:

What in the entire fuck.

My sister always says, "You do too much."

But this time? He did.

And not because he was trying to manipulate me. Because my presence made him believe I was already his.

I wasn't trying to be unforgettable. I was trying to be free.

And when freedom and longing collide . . .

. . . somebody always bleeds.

It wasn't all boys.

There were new songs turned up too loud in cars I didn't belong in.

There were tacos, the kind you eat standing up under neon light, messy and dripping, best when you don't bother with napkins. Spicy, fresh, comforting. That's what those nights tasted like. Permission on a paper plate. Flavor you can't separate from the mess.

Shoes that should've been retired hours ago.

Saying yes because I wanted to.

Laughing too hard with strangers who didn't need my history to hold my joy.

Living unscripted.

Because now I got to choose: What I liked. What I didn't.

What I wanted to taste, touch, and try.

Not from habit. Not out of duty.

Not the version of me shaped by marriage, motherhood, and work. Not the version shaped by fear.

Just me.

Unfiltered. Unmasked. Unapologetically whole. Awkward. Beautiful. Mine.

But it wasn't just the chaos. It was the clarity.

In that messy, glorious in-between, I learned some things.

I like my eggs soft boiled.

I don't like being drunk. But an old-fashioned is hard to turn down.

I like men with nice arms who see women as equals.

I like freedom.

And at night . . . please pass me an edible.

I'm not chasing wild anymore. I'm also not trying to make everything neat.

Because healing doesn't always come wrapped in routines and rituals. Sometimes it comes in sweat and music and mouthfuls of laughter.

In showing up too big—and staying anyway.
In being fully, unapologetically alive.
And yeah, this chapter of my life was ridiculous.
And it was holy.
Because in it, I became someone I'd never met before.

PART VI
The Return to Myself

IF THIS CHAPTER HAD A FLAVOR

Gumbo

IF THIS CHAPTER HAD A SOUNDTRACK

"FLAWLESS (REMIX)"................................ BEYONCÉ FT. NICKI MINAJ

"BAG LADY".. ERYKAH BADU

"I AM LIGHT".. INDIA.ARIE

"TRY".. COLBIE CAILLAT

There wasn't one big, cinematic moment that brought me back to myself. No spotlight. No crescendo. No slow clap in the background.

It happened the way most real things do.

In pieces. In pauses. In private.

It happened in the in-between moments—the ones people skip over in movies. In the car rides where I didn't turn on music because the silence was finally saying something I needed to hear. In the long showers where I cried because it was the only place I could. In the moments I looked in the mirror, not to check my makeup, but to ask myself, "You still in there?"

The journey back to myself didn't start with a plan. It started with a quiet ache. An ache that whispered, *This version of you is tired.* Not just sleepy-tired. *Soul*-tired. From the weight of performing, peacekeeping, pretending.

So I started listening.

This chapter may feel a bit more . . . disjointed than the others. A bit meandering and mixed up. Because what follows isn't a tidy timeline.

It's a trail of breadcrumbs. Moments—hilarious, painful, tender, and wild—that helped me reclaim my voice, my truth, my *self*.

HOPE (AND THE DANGER OF SKIPPING TO THE GOOD PART)

We were in my mom's backyard. It was one of those California days where the sun didn't just shine—it rested on your skin. Warm. Unapologetic. Grounding.

She had her hands in the dirt, whispering to her collard greens like they were sacred—which, in her world, they are.

I was sitting on a cracked patio chair, knees drawn to my chest like I was trying to disappear into myself. Not crying. Not yelling. Just . . . hollow.

I had been trying to hold everything together with optimism and strong coffee. I had been wearing "I'm fine" like a uniform. I had been functioning so well that nobody noticed I was falling apart.

That day, I finally let the quiet spill out.

I told her how exhausted I was—of pretending, of smiling, of being told by well-meaning people that "everything would work out."

And my mama—*Lord.* She doesn't do clichés. She doesn't do spiritual bypasses. She's not about that "just trust" life.

She looked up from the soil—gloves off, forehead glistening—and said:

"Hope is beautiful . . . but not if it makes you ignore what's real."

She said it like she was speaking directly to the root of me.

And something in me split open.

Because I knew exactly what she meant.

I had been gaslighting myself with hope. Telling myself to "stay positive" when what I really needed was to grieve. To feel the loss. To name the anger. To admit that I was hurting.

That moment redefined "hope" for me. Not as blind optimism. Not as performance. But as *presence.*

Real hope doesn't require you to skip the hard part.

It invites you to stay with it. To hold the pain in one hand and the possibility in the other. To say, *I see how bad it is. And I still believe in better.*

That day, sitting next to my mother and her collards, I didn't suddenly become whole. But I did stop lying to myself.

And sometimes . . . that's where the healing starts.

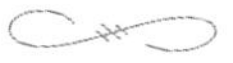

Still, there are moments when something more cracks through.

When softness shows up in ways you can't explain. When the unseen speaks louder than logic.

One of those moments came four months after my Auntie Margo passed.

She had battled cancer for years—quietly, stylishly, with a strength you didn't question. She planned her own funeral like a final masterpiece. Elegant. Intentional. Complete.

She asked me to speak at her service.

I stood in front of a room full of people who adored her, and I opened with words borrowed from her beloved Prince:

"Dearly beloved, we are gathered here today to get through this thing called life."

It was the perfect sentence. The kind of thing only Auntie Margo could make feel like both a joke and a prayer.

She was larger than life, but realer than real. Crop tops in the summer. Statement jewelry at Thanksgiving. Radio voice and sharp wit. She showed up in casseroles, in texts, in the way she could side-eye you and love you at the same time. She taught me that presence was the purest form of love.

So I wasn't surprised when she showed up again. Just . . . humbled.

My cousin Ferris and I had both bought tickets to a Tyler Henry show without telling each other. If you don't know, Tyler Henry is a medium. A Hollywood psychic. The kind that makes you feel and question everything in the same breath.

The venue wasn't big. Mostly white. Maybe fifteen hundred people. Tyler did about seven readings that night. And in the second-to-last, he paused and said,

"I see this beautiful brown-skinned woman smiling. She has this radiant smile."

Ferris and I looked at each other—we already knew.

Then he asked,

"Does anyone know a Margo?"

Not an energy. Not a symbol. A name.

A woman raised her hand. "My name is Margo."

Tyler tilted his head.

"No . . . this is an *Auntie Margo*."

By that time, we had made it to the mic.

He told us she was there—with our grandmother, Juanita, and our other aunt, Arnita. All named. All accounted for.

He said they were giddy. Laughing. Full of light. No warnings. No lessons. Just love.

And I knew at that moment . . . if anyone could send a message from the afterlife just to say, "Baby, I'm good"—it would be the women in my family.

Hope, *real hope*, doesn't live in certainty.

It lives in the flicker. The whisper. The moment where you decide to believe anyway—even if no one else gets it.

I used to think "hope" meant ignoring the pain. Now I know it means refusing to be defined by it.

I used to think "being realistic" meant preparing for disappointment. Now I know it means making space for mystery.

Hope isn't about skipping to the good part.

It's about staying soft in the hard part—and trusting that goodness can still meet you there.

COOL WAS A CAGE (AND I WAS GOOD AT WEARING IT)

There's this game we all learn to play, whether we realize it or not.

The game of looking okay.

The rules are simple: Be clever, not clear. Be witty, not soft. Be polished, not present.

I knew how to play. I was *good* at it.

It started online—like everything does now. You post something soft . . . something *real* . . . something that costs you a little skin to say out loud.

It lands like a feather in the algorithm. Maybe two likes. A pity emoji. Silence.

But then? Post something sarcastic. Throw in a well-timed eye roll or a spicy meme?

Now it's engagement. *Now* you're relevant.

I felt it, that subtle pull to stay performative. To be digestible. Funny. Breezy.

Because that gets rewarded. And when you've spent your life earning your keep through usefulness, performance feels familiar. Almost like safety.

But the deeper truth?

Every time I turned the volume down on my sincerity . . . I was turning the volume down on me.

It was in one of those late-night scrolls, drowning in curated detachment, that the question appeared, right there in my feed:

If you lose yourself for applause, what exactly are they clapping for?

That line haunted me.

So I stopped chasing "clever" and started telling the truth again.

Sometimes it didn't land. Sometimes it did.

But every time, it sounded like me. It reminded me of what my mom told me in the garden: *Hope is only beautiful if it doesn't ignore what's real.* Truth is the same way. It has to sound like you, or it's just performance. And if it's a performance, who exactly are you performing for?

BRACED: WHEN CALM IS A COSTUME

I've been thinking about what it means to live in a constant state of *ready.*

Not prepared. Not open. Braced.

For years I've clung to the sentiment that every raindrop is not a storm. I can live with that because I've always had an umbrella nearby. But some of my friends? They've been caught in the rain too many times without one. Now they clutch it tight at the mere mention of rain in the forecast.

That's the difference. For me, rain feels like bloom. For them, a siren.

It's the kind of stance you adopt when life teaches you

early that safety isn't guaranteed. When survival becomes a personality trait. When your nervous system gets trained to scan for threat before it ever scans for joy.

Some people grow up that way . . . too small in houses too loud, the only softness in a hard environment. They become fighters. They get good at it. They survive, achieve, even thrive—at least by the world's standards.

But underneath all that resilience is a question that lingers: *How do you rest when you've never felt safe?*

Because sometimes all that hard work still doesn't buy the deep breath you deserve. The armor stays on. Everyone's an opp. Rest feels risky.

And maybe, over time, the fight becomes familiar. Comfortable, even. Maybe it becomes . . . you.

Maybe it's easier to stay ready than to figure out who you are without the vigilance.

But then there are people like me—people who've regulated themselves into a curated sense of calm. People who pursue peace at all costs. Who avoid conflict like it's contagious. Who shut down, smile, walk away, or retreat into logic just to keep the waters still.

We think we're doing better. But we're not always doing well.

I've let go of relationships that were salvageable because conflict made me flinch. I've performed peace while internally screaming. I've convinced myself I was grounded when really . . . I was just frozen.

And maybe what I'm learning is . . . we're not opposites. We're mirrors.

One of us needs to exhale. The other needs to *roar*.

Maybe the goal isn't to pick a side, but to learn when to soften and when to stand. When to put the armor down and when to pick it up.

Because balance isn't passive. It's not the absence of tension. It's the presence of intention.

And nobody gets to opt out of the work.

TO BE BRILLIANT AND STILL WRONG

I've always been smart.

That's not ego—it's observation. I've been praised for my mind for as long as I can remember. Quick thinker. Sharp strategist. Queen of the five-step plan.

I used to think that was enough.

That if I was smart enough, I could out-think disappointment. That if I was resourceful enough, I could protect myself from heartbreak. That if I was helpful enough, I could earn my place in every room.

But here's what nobody tells you:

You can be brilliant . . . and still be completely wrong. You can be logical . . . and still be disconnected from your own life.

I've built systems that ran like clockwork and collapsed from the inside. I've solved problems with precision and never paused to ask, "What's this really about?"

Being intelligent doesn't mean you're awake. And performing stability isn't the same as being grounded.

The moment that shifted everything for me wasn't loud. It was in the middle of a Tuesday. I was writing an email—some quick fix for something I didn't care about—when I stopped and thought:

I am solving things I don't even believe in.

It wasn't burnout. It was misalignment. And no amount of "brilliance" can fix that.

At that moment, I didn't know it yet, but everything was shifting inside. That day was the beginning of a new chapter, one where I gave myself permission to stop performing usefulness. To trade being right for being real. Of course, permission doesn't always look graceful. Before I could integrate that shift, something in me still had to break down. Which is how I found myself in the kitchen, weeping over a broken can opener.

THE CAN OPENER AND THE WOMAN WHO SNAPPED

I cried for an hour because the can opener broke.

Not because I was hungry. Not because I was having a rough day. Not even because I needed what was in the can.

It was because something in me . . . gave out.

No screams, just the soft, humiliating clink of a dull metal blade failing to pierce a can of black beans.

That's all it took.

I stood in my kitchen—barefoot, in a sweatshirt with sleeves too long, mascara tear-smudged from whatever the hell emotions I had shoved down that week—and stared at that stupid can opener like it had personally, deliberately betrayed me.

And then I wept.

Not a cute cry. Not the kind you wipe away with a sleeve and keep pushing through. I cried like my body had been holding that grief in reserve, for when it was safe to let it out.

When you grow up in performance mode, you get good at holding it together.

You pride yourself on staying calm under pressure. Rational. Resourceful. Easy to love.

You become a master of the steady voice. The patient tone. The high-functioning smile. You know how to get through a crisis without raising your voice or raising suspicion.

The breakdown doesn't come when it "makes sense." It doesn't happen at the funeral, or during the layoff, or after the breakup.

No.

It sneaks up on a Tuesday. In your kitchen. With a can opener.

Because the body always keeps score. And mine . . . had reached its limit.

That night was the first time I realized I wasn't just sad. I wasn't tired. I wasn't sensitive.

I was angry.

Angry that I had carried so much without complaint. Angry that my peacekeeping had cost me my voice. Angry that somewhere along the way, I'd learned to equate being lovable with being quiet.

That night didn't make me whole.

But it introduced me to a version of myself I'd been ignoring.

I've been getting to know her ever since.

SPIDER-MAN AND STILLNESS

This weekend, I found peace . . . tucked neatly inside Spider-Man onesie pajamas that once belonged to my son.

I wear my kids' old clothes often. Their six-foot-something frames stretch out hoodies and sweatpants that now hang off my shoulders and pool around my ankles. And yet, every oversized sleeve feels like a warm embrace—familiar, safe, loved.

As I zipped myself into that well-worn onesie, I felt a wave of something I hadn't been able to access all week: peace.

Not the kind of peace that comes from everything going right. Not the kind that requires silence or solitude or a perfectly curated day.

This peace was quieter. Subtler. Rooted.

It came from gratitude.

I'd been thinking about how much I adore my kids—not

just as a parent, but as a person. I mean I thoroughly enjoy these humans. They make me laugh, make me think, and keep me grounded. They're not just my children . . . they are my favorite people, and that's not hyperbole. It's backed by an obnoxious number of group texts, FaceTimes, inside jokes, and "I just wanted to tell you this real quick" phone calls.

In those moments of thinking about them, about how lucky I am to be their mom . . . I feel still.

Gratitude slows everything down. It brings the focus away from what's missing and back to what's here.

Peace doesn't always announce itself. Sometimes it shows up disguised as a flash of "thanks." A small pause. A breath that goes all the way down.

I used to chase peace like it was a destination . . . something I'd find after the to-do list was done, after the world quieted down.

But peace doesn't wait to show up at the end of effort. It rests, always, at the center of appreciation.

And sometimes . . . it hides in a Spider-Man onesie.

SOMETIMES SURVIVAL WINS

I wish I could say reclaiming myself always looked like freedom. Like walking out of meetings head high, voice steady, boundary set. But sometimes, it looked like a whisper.

Like biting my tongue.

Like smiling through something I didn't agree with because, well, rent was due.

I've learned that authenticity is not always convenient.

It's beautiful. Powerful. Liberating. But it's not always practical.

That's what nobody tells you when they shout "be yourself" across LinkedIn.

They don't ask if you can afford it.

When I was nineteen, I got fired.

I went home. No kids, no bills, no fallout. It was a bruise to the ego, but that was all.

Now?

A misstep doesn't just hit me. It hits my household. It means paused tuition payments. Missed copays. The whole house feeling my fear.

I had to learn to wear the mask—

Not as deception, but as protection.

My dad did it too. Suited up in a white-coded voice, smiling just right, sealing the deal.

Then he'd come home and laugh about how well it worked.

He wasn't confused. He knew the game.

And now, so do I.

Here's the part I had to forgive myself for: Choosing survival doesn't mean I abandoned myself. It means I protected her.

Kept her safe until it was okay to bring her out again.

I know the difference now.

Between who I am . . .

. . . and who I sometimes have to be.

And that, too, is wisdom.

OPTIONS ARE OXYGEN

Not long ago, a single comment—sharp, dismissive, delivered with just the right amount of indifference—could've undone me.

Sent me into that quiet spiral where the weight of "being professional" feels indistinguishable from being *trapped.*

Trapped by expectations. By responsibility. By the illusion of choice . . . when survival is on the line.

But this time? Same tone. Same energy.

And I didn't flinch.

Not because I've become unbothered (though . . . goals). Because something inside me had shifted.

A few weeks ago, I had no exit strategy. Just grit and bills.

Now?

I've got a plan. A vision. Options.

And let me tell you—options are oxygen.

Let's not pretend options aren't a privilege. They absolutely are.

I'm not just talking about well-funded, well-connected privilege.

I'm talking about the kind of plan born from imagination and audacity. From believing that 1 percent better can get you there. From a reframe so rooted in self-worth it lets you say: *That's mine*—with your chest.

Like a kid pointing at a Bentley and saying, "That's my car."

So ask yourself:

Am I the kind of person who internalizes disrespect from someone clearly out of their depth?

Or am I the kind of person who knows—deep in my bones—I could literally never?

Because how we react? Isn't just about what's said to us. It's about who we are when we hear it.

When you're stuck, everything feels heavier.

But when you've got direction—even if you're still in the same room—you move differently. You breathe differently. You hold power differently.

So maybe the question in hard moments isn't always "How do I fix this?"

Maybe it's "Who do I need to become to carry this with less effort?"

You don't have to escape today. But maybe you can become the version of you who knows how.

And that . . . changes everything.

FAITH, CURVED SPACE, AND THE UNSEEN

I didn't expect a spiritual experience at a science lecture.

I went to see Neil deGrasse Tyson because I wanted to feel smart again. I had spent so much time navigating emotions, uncertainty, people—I wanted data. Logic. A break from the messiness of the human heart.

But somewhere between his breakdown of dark energy and the curvature of space-time, I found myself . . . humbled.

Because what he was describing—these invisible forces, these unseen dimensions, these elegant unknowns—sounded an awful lot like faith.

Not the kind you find in church. The kind that lives in gut feelings. In late-night prayers you're not sure anyone hears. In the way your spirit rises when there's no proof, only knowing.

Astrophysics, it turns out, is just faith with a whiteboard.

We trust gravity without seeing it. We believe in energies we can't touch. We speak confidently about dimensions we've never visited with more conviction than we give our own intuition.

And I thought, *Why do we apologize for believing in the unseen?*

Why do we feel silly for trusting ourselves when scientists do it all the time?

I walked out of that theater different.

Not because I had new answers. But because I remembered: The world is big enough to hold mystery. And so am I.

GHANA: THE DAY MY VOICE FOUND ITS ECHO

It started with a man.

Well . . . a date.

One of those low-lit, medium-potential evenings where the conversation dips just deep enough to be interesting, but not so deep that you forget you're still screening for red flags.

We were trading travel stories when he tilted his head and asked, "Do you travel just for fun . . . or with purpose?"

I smiled. Pretended it didn't land in my chest like a dare. Said something breezy in the moment. Laughed it off.

But it followed me home. Because the truth?

Most of my travel had been escape.

From burnout. From heartbreak. From routine.

From myself, if I'm honest.

So when the opportunity came to volunteer abroad, I said *yes*.

Not to save anyone.

But because I needed to find something—someone—in myself.

Ghana was heat and color and rhythm.

It smelled like sun and spice.

It moved with a cadence that made me slow down in ways I didn't know how to back home.

The first week was tourist stuff. Woven baskets. Market greetings. Drums teaching my chest how to breathe again. Eating banku with my hands, that fermented blend of cornmeal and cassava, rolled and dipped into a spicy tomato and fish stew. It was sour and tangy, earthy and alive, the kind of flavor that stays on your tongue long after the bite is gone.

It reminded me of gumbo back home. Not in taste, but

in spirit. Both are mixed pots of survival and story, dishes you can't rush because they carry too much history in them. Gumbo is soul food stitched together from scraps, layered slowly until it becomes something whole. Banku and stew was the same, a lesson in how cultures fold their trials and triumphs into food. How what's on the plate is never just what's on the plate.

But the second week?

That's when it shifted.

I was teaching at a small school where the computers were more wish than reality. Their textbooks were older than some of the kids.

I walked in ready to talk about email or Excel. But when I asked what they wanted to learn, a girl raised her hand and asked, "How does Facebook work?"

And I swear it hit like scripture.

Not because it was hard to answer.

But because I saw her. Not just as a student—but as *me*.

Curious. Capable.

Hungry for understanding.

Deserving of access.

So I taught.

Sweaty and wide-eyed, I drew crude diagrams on the chalkboard. Talked about packets and data flow. Networks and backends.

I used metaphors I'd picked up in startup war rooms and tech briefings.

And then—

—a girl, maybe sixteen, raised her hand again and asked,

"When I type my password, how does it not get stolen?"

I paused.

Not because I didn't know. But because at that moment, I realized—she *gets* it. She was tracking. Connecting dots.

And just then, a boy in the back asked, "Is that . . . a job?"

My throat tightened. Because there it was.

The moment I didn't know I'd been traveling toward.

That question cracked something open.

Not just in them. In me.

I saw what they needed. I saw what I had been carrying all along. It wasn't just knowledge they wanted. It wasn't just social media savvy and how to farm engagement or get followers.

It was access.

It was proof.

Proof that someone like *me* could stand in front of them and say:

"You belong in this too."

I came back to the States with red dust on my shoes and a fire under my ribs.

I raised money. Collected equipment. And I returned—this time, with laptops, software, and a promise: *You don't have to be from Silicon Valley to belong in it.*

That trip didn't change everything. But it changed *me*.

It was the first time I used my voice not just to explain, but to open a door.

I've been looking for doors ever since.

THE LUBE WASN'T FANCY. THE PANIC WAS REAL.

Let me tell you what *didn't* happen.

This wasn't some sensual, candlelit moment with rose petals and a perfectly curated playlist. There were no silk sheets. No gentle whispers. No cosmic alignment.

There was a ceiling fan humming like a broken engine, a light too bright to be flattering, and the distinct hum of a grown woman trying to make her body cooperate.

Because menopause? Yeah. She doesn't care about your vibe.

She shows up uninvited. Dry, itchy, unpredictable. Like, "Oh, you thought you were still thirty-five? That's cute."

So that night, I was prepared—not for passion, but for prevention.

I had bought a water-based lube at the drugstore. Nothing fancy. No sleek branding. Just a quiet label promising "comfort," which is all I really wanted. Comfort. Hydration. And maybe, if the stars aligned . . . a good time.

And listen, for a while, things went as planned. We did what adults do when the chemistry is right and the moment is warming up. I even remember thinking, *Okay, maybe this isn't so bad. Maybe I'm not completely falling apart.*

But then . . . after . . .

I sat up. Stretched. Shifted. And noticed something.

Crumbs.

Sex crumbs.

On me. On him. On the sheets.

Like someone had quietly eaten a flakey scone on our bodies while I wasn't looking.

For one breathless moment, I panicked.

Like, deep, irrational, sweaty-palmed panic.

I wasn't confused—I was mortified. My brain spun into full disaster mode: *What is happening? Is my body disintegrating? Did I shed something? Did he shed something? Is this a medical emergency? Am I—oh my God—am I flaking?!*

I didn't say anything at first. Just froze.

The man? Calm. Unfazed. Like maybe this was . . . a thing that happens?

Which somehow made it worse.

I couldn't get comfortable. Couldn't rest. Couldn't sleep. Every time I shifted, I felt the crinkle of betrayal on the sheets. I laid there, eyes wide, soul spiraling, thinking:

I can never see this man again. I need to delete my number from his phone. I wonder how much it costs to move to a new city under a different name.

I didn't laugh. Not at first. I was too busy trying to figure out if this was early-onset body glitter or the physical manifestation of my last shred of dignity.

Eventually—hours later, maybe even the next morning—I googled it.

Turns out? That affordable, menopause-approved lube? Dries down into crumbs. Literal flakes. Residue. A trail of humiliation.

That's when I finally laughed.

Not because it was funny. But because the alternative was to cry over something so wildly human that my younger self would've crumbled beneath it.

But I didn't crumble.

Not really.

Because now? Now I can say it:

Yes, I am mid-menopause. Yes, I am finding my way back to myself, even as my hormones keep trying to ghost me. Yes, I had sex and left behind evidence that could double as trail markers in a wicked witch bedtime story.

And yes—I lived.

And I learned.

That reclaiming your body after forty is both hilarious and holy. That, sometimes, healing comes after panic. That the real flex is laughing after you've imagined changing your name and going into witness protection.

The lube wasn't fancy. The moment wasn't graceful.

But that lesson? That lesson was everything.

Because this body—flaky, fire-hot, tender, transforming—is still mine.

And I'm still here.

STILL SOMEBODY'S BABY

What a blessing it is: to still get to rest in the youth of being someone's niece, baby sister, daughter, or younger cousin.

To still be cared for and nurtured, even in adulthood. In late adulthood. In your mid-forties, where "grown" waves at you with hot flashes and responsibilities.

When youth starts to feel more like a memory than a moment, it's easy to forget that being held isn't just for children.

But that's the beauty of a big family.

This weekend, I spent time with my cousin. She's much younger than I am—closer in age to my kids than to me. We're the same number of years apart as my mom and I.

And still . . . she lets me play friend. I get to weave in and out of lanes usually reserved for aunts and parents—offering advice, cracking jokes, and slipping soft life lessons between laughs.

And her parents? They offer me the same tenderness. The same care, wrapped in small but sacred gestures:

"Text me when you land."

"You need anything before your drive back?"

That kind of tenderness reminds me that I'm still somebody's baby too.

That's the gift of a big family.

You get to be both the caregiver and the cared-for. You get to pour in—and be poured into. You get to wipe tears—and still have someone offer you a tissue.

There's something powerful—holy, even—about resting in both roles.

It reminds you: *No matter how grown you get, you're never too old to be wrapped in love.*

That kind of love? It doesn't age out.

WHAT THE BREADCRUMBS GAVE ME

These stories? They weren't loud. They didn't demand a plot twist or an applause break.

But they brought me home.

Not all at once. Not with certainty. Just . . . one little breadcrumb at a time.

A sigh in a onesie. A flinch that never came. The half-laughed panic of midlife intimacy. A cracked joke while quietly unraveling. A reminder that I am still—even now—somebody's baby.

I used to think healing would look like a breakthrough. A clear "before" and "after." A moment big enough to finally announce: *I'm finally okay.*

Now I know healing is quieter than that. It's fragments gathered and stitched into something whole. It's the onesie. The voice that does not rise. The plan that lets you exhale. The tissue someone offers you just because.

When I need to ground—to, once again, return to myself—it's these small moments I call on. The lessons that came not from striving, but from listening, first to the world, and finally to me.

These moments didn't rescue me. They reminded and remembered me. Called me back to the parts I thought I'd outgrown or lost. They whispered, *Start here.*

You are already enough.

Healing is a trail. And every breadcrumb matters.

PART VII
A Devotion to the Woman I Am

IF THIS CHAPTER HAD A FLAVOR

Fluffy pancakes

IF THIS CHAPTER HAD A SOUNDTRACK

"LEVEL UP"	CIARA
"GOOD AS HELL"	LIZZO
"RISE UP"	ANDRA DAY
"COFFEE"	SYLVAN ESSO
"BLESSED"	JILL SCOTT

There's a kind of love I didn't understand until recently. Not the breathless, butterflies kind. Not the kind that makes you forget to eat or texts you *good morning*. Not even the fierce, mama-bear love I've always given to my people, my tribe, my kids.

This love is different.

It's quieter. Grown. Rooted. The kind my mom showed

me years ago when she brought home a bunny on Easter morning, not with chaos or applause, but with wood, wire, and the rabbit hutch she built herself. Love that's soft and spirited, but steady enough to hold. The kind that shows up at 6 a.m. when the alarm goes off and those first thoughts emerge: *Can I handle another day of this? Do I feel like it?*

It's the love that responds with, *Yes. Because I promised myself I would.*

It's in the supplements I take, even when they taste like chalk. In the protein I prep, the gym sessions I show up for, the pills I line up each morning like a prayer.

I used to wait for clarity to come in big, cinematic waves. Now, I find the divine in small consistency.

The truth is . . . I have become someone I can trust.

There was a time—recent, actually—when I was constantly fixing myself. Every goal had a deadline. Every body part had a critique. Every choice was a strategy: *How does this move me forward? How does this make me better?*

It was easy to confuse the grind for growth. But that wasn't healing. It was hustling. It was performance clothed in "self-improvement."

I wasn't resting. I was rebranding.

Now?

Now I treat myself like someone worth staying with.

It's like pancakes, simple, circular, forgiving. You don't need a holiday or an audience. Just a skillet and a little care. Flipped one at a time, stacked until you have enough. Pancakes are proof that consistency is its own kind of devotion. They've always been my comfort food, a soft return on a plate. That's what this chapter of my life feels like: not a reinvention, but a stack of small, steady choices that remind me I'm worth showing up for.

That's what hormone therapy was for me. Not a last resort. Not a desperate fix.

It was a love letter to my future self. The one who deserves clarity. Energy. Rest that actually restores. The one who doesn't want to white-knuckle her way through another hot flash or foggy morning.

I didn't start this journey because I was broken. I started because I wanted to feel whole again.

Not the old me. Not the hustling me. The wise me. The *well* me.

It didn't happen overnight. The first time I applied the creams, it felt . . . awkward. Mechanical. But also intimate. Like an anointing. Like I was finally tending to the parts of me I had ignored—not because I was lazy, but because I was taught to be strong.

And this—this softness? This willingness to treat fatigue like a signal, not a flaw? This is my new strength.

The gym used to be where I went to punish myself. Now, it's where I go to remember.

That I can move with power. That I can lift heavy things and not call them burdens. That I can sweat and not call it struggle. That I can show up for myself not because I'm behind—but because I'm worthy.

I don't chase outcomes anymore. I honor the ritual.

Lacing up the shoes. Filling the water bottle. Pressing play on the playlist. Starting the warm-up.

These small acts? They are my devotion.

And rest?

Rest isn't what happens when I collapse. It's what I schedule so collapse doesn't get the chance.

It's in my calendar now. A standing meeting with God. Because I deserve to be well. Not just "not sick." Not just "managing."

Well. Clear. Cared for. Held—by me.

Here's something I didn't expect: I haven't weighed myself in a month.

Not because I'm "trusting the process." Not because I forgot. Because I stopped caring like I used to.

Not careless. Just . . . peaceful.

I started tracking different data points: How I feel in my skin. How my breath moves. How I sleep. How I walk past a mirror without holding my breath.

The scale used to be my morning gospel. I've cried over half a pound. Punished myself for water weight. Chased numbers like they held the key to worthiness.

But now?

Now I choose softness over obsession.

And still—because I am human—I know I'll probably step on that scale again one day. Maybe tomorrow. Maybe next week. Maybe because I think my jeans feel tighter and I want proof I'm not unraveling.

And when that happens?

I may flinch. I may spiral. And then . . . I will breathe.

Because the point isn't to be perfect. It's to be present. To know how to come back to myself, over and over again.

That's the real love story now.

Not a number. Not a plan. Not a macro split or before-and-after pic.

The romance is how I treat myself in the in-between.

When the gym feels hard. When I miss a day (or five). When I eat for comfort, not macros. When I cry after doing everything "right" and still feel off.

The devotion is in the return. The decision to stay in a relationship with myself, even when I'm annoyed, tired, or tender.

I don't ghost myself anymore. I don't punish the parts of me that need grace. I hold them. I listen. I adjust.

And I know: This love will evolve.

My rituals will change. My rhythms will shift. My needs will grow louder or softer depending on the season I'm in.

And that's okay.

Because this is the kind of love I want in every part of my life: Soft. Consistent. Curious.

Unbothered by perfection. Devoted to truth.

This chapter of my life is quiet. But don't confuse that with boring.

There is revolution in how I rise now. There is protest in my boundaries. There is poetry in how I prep my meals, refill my supplements, and protect my peace.

And if I ever forget—when I slip back into overworking or shrinking or spiraling—

I know the way back.

Because I built it.

Because I laid the bricks myself. With rest. And grace.

And patience.

Because I finally understand:

Soft doesn't mean weak. Consistency doesn't mean rigid. And healing doesn't always mean becoming someone new—because ultimately, the best form of "becoming" is returning. It's remembering who you've always been underneath the noise.

Loving myself didn't mean I stopped asking questions. It meant I started asking better ones.

Not the ones that sound like judgment: *Why can't you just stick to it? What's wrong with you? Why are you like this?*

But the ones that sound like care: *What do you need today? Where does this tightness come from? What story are you believing right now?*

Because devotion without self-awareness is just performance. And I don't want a life that's beautiful on the outside but hollow inside.

So I check in.

When I feel off . . . I pause.

I get curious.

I investigate gently.

Sometimes the answer is simple. *Hunger. Sleep. Hormones.*

But sometimes . . . It's a boundary I betrayed. A truth I swallowed. A part of me asking not to be ignored.

This is the part of the journey that doesn't come with applause.

There's no montage. No dramatic climax. Just a series of quiet moments where I choose to stay in a relationship with myself.

To ask, *What's really going on?*

Because the anxiety I blame on my to-do list might actually be grief. Or a no I swallowed instead of spitting out. Or the little girl in me who still thinks she has to earn her rest.

So if you're reading this, and you feel off—but don't know why?

Pause.

Don't perform. Don't punish. Just *ask*.

Ask gently. Listen honestly. Answer slowly.

That feeling you're having? That edge you can't name?

It's not your failure. It's your signal.

And if you follow it inward . . . if you're brave enough to be still with it, soft enough to not demand it make sense too soon, and curious enough to believe your body's not betraying you?

It just might lead you home.

Home to your breath. To your truth. To the version of you that never needed fixing—just remembering.

And maybe, if you follow it far enough . . .

It might just lead you back to Amazonia.

Where softness is power. Where resilience wears lipstick and sweat. Where the women who raised you still whisper, "You got this, baby."

And you do. Because you always have.

by Mya Fort-Marshall.

EPILOGUE

You made it to the end of this book, and you're probably wondering . . . what did I just read?

I get it. It's a lot.

But remember—this book is not a manual.

It's not self-help. It's not even a memoir.

It's a friend.

It's a late-night conversation with someone who talks too much . . . and occasionally drops a gem or two.

It's a reflection, in the purest sense.

If you saw even a sliver of yourself in these pages—maybe that's the point.

And if this book is a mirror . . . I hope you liked what you saw.

BREADCRUMBS

The Whole Damn Loaf

These weren't big revelations. They were moments. Quiet ones. Uncomfortable ones. The kind that land in your chest before your head catches up.

Here's what they left behind:

PART I: WHO RAISED YOU—PIRATES?

- Even the wildest nicknames can be love letters.
- Resilience isn't always built from trauma—sometimes it's passed down in laughter, rituals, and sourdough.
- Sensitivity and sarcasm are both survival skills.
- You don't have to inherit everything. You get to edit the story.
- You were already enough before the world asked you to shrink.

PART II: BECOMING ON BRACE AVE.

- Identity doesn't need permission. If you're living it, it's valid.
- Community can be built—sometimes from scratch, sometimes over spaghetti.
- Safety isn't just physical. It's emotional.
- The right pivot can change everything.
- Even the weirdest parts of you are worthy of being witnessed.

PART III: MOTHERHOOD, MARRIAGE, AND THE GREAT UNRAVELING

- Parenting isn't performance. It's presence.
- Love shouldn't ask you to disappear.
- Unraveling is just truth shedding its costume.
- Grief doesn't always wail. Sometimes it goes to work.
- Let people care for you. Rest is not a reward.
- The shape of family can change. Love doesn't expire.

PART IV: NARRATIVE IS INHERITANCE

- The stories we're told shape us. So do the ones we choose to believe.
- Presence and absence both leave fingerprints.
- Grace is a valid plot twist.

- You don't have to villainize someone to heal.
- Legacy can be soft and still be strong.

PART V: THE MESSY IN-BETWEEN

- Sometimes survival gives you a second body—and a second chance.
- The glow-up can be covered by insurance. Don't waste it.
- Healing doesn't always look holy. Sometimes it looks like table dancing and edibles.
- It's okay to say yes without a spreadsheet.
- Curiosity isn't recklessness—it's reclamation.
- You don't owe anyone the polished version.
- Soft-boiled eggs. Nice arms. Freedom. And at night . . . please pass the edible.
- You are allowed to change. Radically. Without apology.

PART VI: THE RETURN TO MYSELF

- Hope doesn't skip the hard part. It sits in it with you.
- Cool is a cage. And performance will starve you slowly.
- Calm isn't always peace.
- A failed can opener can open up rage. Let it.
- Gratitude is a grounding practice.
- Survival isn't shameful. It's sacred.
- Options are oxygen.

- Belief doesn't always carry a Bible. Sometimes it sounds like science.
- Purpose might sneak up disguised as service.
- Midlife panic is still holy. (Even with sex crumbs.)
- You're never too grown to be wrapped in love.
- Healing is a breadcrumb trail. Follow it.

PART VII: A DEVOTION TO THE WOMAN I AM

- Discipline is how you prove you've got your own back.
- Healing might look like a routine. Or a boundary. Or doing nothing.
- You don't have to fix yourself. Just stay with yourself.
- Softness isn't surrender—it's skill.
- The return is the point.
- You're allowed to ask better questions.
- Wholeness isn't a finish line. It's a remembering.

FINAL THOUGHT

Breadcrumbs aren't just proof you survived the journey. They're reminders that you've been walking yourself home the whole time. So if you forget who you are, don't panic. Just start there.

You've been leaving yourself clues.

POSTSCRIPT

Recipes & Rituals

Music is memory. Flavor is story. And healing? That lives in both.

These aren't just songs and meals. Each one is tied to a chapter of this book, folded into moments of grief, joy, growth, identity, survival, and return. These were the sounds playing in the background while I unraveled . . . and the flavors that reminded me who I was when I came back to myself.

You don't have to make every recipe or cue up every track. Just know: They were created with presence, intention, and a little bit of rebellion. And they were made with you in mind.

PART I
Who Raised You—Pirates?

PLAYLIST

"HORSES"	RICKIE LEE JONES
"ADORE"	PRINCE
"NEVER TOO MUCH"	LUTHER VANDROSS
"CAUGHT UP IN THE RAPTURE"	ANITA BAKER
"FOR THE LOVE OF MONEY"	THE O'JAYS
"HIS EYE IS ON THE SPARROW"	WHITNEY HOUSTON (LAURYN HILL AND TANYA BLOUNT VERSION)

Grandma's Butter Rolls

(AKA GRANDMA'S SOFT ARMOR)

We loved a sweet treat at my grandmother's house. She was a skilled baker, known for selling cakes and pies during the holidays. Everyone had their favorite: Aunt Arnita loved her yellow cake with chocolate frosting; Aunt Melinda claimed the coconut cake, snowy white and piled with shavings, as hers.

Me? I always gravitated toward the humble treats born out of limited resources and pure creativity. Cinnamon sugar toast. And my absolute favorite: butter rolls.

Cinnamon Sugar Toast you already know . . . bread, butter, sugar, cinnamon. Instant joy. But butter rolls? They were less common, more magical. The ingredients are simple: flour, sugar, cinnamon, butter, milk, and eggs . . . pantry staples that could become something decadent. I've since learned they're cousins to the Depression-era "sugar pie," what Martha Stewart once called a "desperation pie" because it was made when fresh fruit wasn't available.

Traditional butter rolls bake in a sweet milk bath. But my grandma had her own twist: She poured the cream over after the rolls had already crisped in the oven. The result? Crispy edges softened by a silky sauce that sank into every bite. Comfort disguised as dessert. Love disguised as sweetness.

DOUGH

- 2 cups all-purpose flour
- 1 tbsp sugar
- 1 tsp baking powder
- ½ tsp salt
- 6 tbsp cold butter, cubed
- ¾ cup milk

FILLING

- ½ cup softened butter
- ½ cup sugar
- 1 tbsp cinnamon

MILK SAUCE

- 2 cups whole milk
- ½ cup sugar
- 1 tsp vanilla
- Pinch of nutmeg
- 2 tbsp butter

MAKE IT

1. Preheat the oven to 375°F.
2. In a bowl, mix flour, sugar, baking powder, and salt. Cut in cold butter until crumbly. Stir in milk to form a soft dough.
3. Roll dough into a rectangle. Divide into 4 pieces. Spread with softened butter, sprinkle with sugar and cinnamon. Crimp edges with fork to secure shut.
4. Place rolls in a greased baking dish. Bake for 18–22 minutes until golden.
5. Meanwhile, warm the milk, sugar, vanilla, nutmeg, and butter until sugar dissolves.
6. Pour the hot sauce over the baked rolls and let it soak in.

PART II
Becoming on Brace Ave.

PLAYLIST

"PEOPLE EVERYDAY" .... ARRESTED DEVELOPMENT

"KEEP YA HEAD UP" 2PAC

"'93 'TIL INFINITY" .... SOULS OF MISCHIEF

"GIRLS JUST WANT TO HAVE FUN" .... CYNDI LAUPER

"DOO WOP (THAT THING)" .... LAURYN HILL

Muffaletta Grilled Cheese

(AKA THE ECLECTIC KITCHEN)

Life on Brace Street elevated my palate. My mother made dishes my grandmother never even heard of, and her love for food was international. Our Sunday mornings were spent in bed with cooking shows—our version of devotion. I still remember watching her attempt Julia Child's duck à l'orange one Thanksgiving, determined to bring French cuisine into our small kitchen.

But our refrigerator told a different story. It didn't mirror our culinary interests so much as our curiosity.

We were condiment-rich—sauces, spreads, jars of olives and pickles—well ahead of the charcuterie craze.

So I learned to piece things together. Sweet, salty, savory. A little improvisation, a little invention. The Muffaletta Grilled Cheese was born that way—the creation of a young girl who learned that an eclectic kitchen could still satisfy an evolving palate.

INGREDIENTS

- 2 slices sourdough bread
- 2–3 slices brie cheese (or mozzarella if you prefer mild)
- Thin slices of apple (Granny Smith or Honeycrisp)
- Olive tapenade (or a handful of chopped olives)
- Peach jam (or fig preserves, if you're fancy)
- Butter for grilling

MAKE IT

1. Butter the outside of both bread slices.
2. On the inside, spread one slice with olive tapenade and the other with peach jam.
3. Layer brie slices and apple in between, then sandwich together.
4. Grill in a skillet over medium heat until golden brown on both sides and the cheese is melty.

SERVE WARM. Eat it cross-legged on the floor, or with a paper towel instead of a plate. This sandwich tastes like resourcefulness—the reminder that even a condiment-rich fridge can create a feast.

PART III
Motherhood, Marriage, and the Great Unraveling

PLAYLIST

"TO ZION"	LAURYN HILL
"EX-FACTOR"	LAURYN HILL
"BUTTERFLY"	MARIAH CAREY
"THIS WOMAN'S WORK"	MAXWELL
"GOLDEN"	JILL SCOTT

Mac & Anointing

(AKA THE HOLY SIDE DISH)

I don't mean to brag or anything, but my ex-husband asked me to send *MY* mac and cheese to his house for Thanksgiving. That's high praise in Black culture—you don't just get assigned the mac and cheese unless your dish has earned reverence.

This recipe was born from small tweaks over the years and, oddly enough, history lessons. Did you know baked mac and cheese was introduced to the US by James Hemings, the enslaved chef of Thomas Jefferson? Jefferson sent Hemings to France in 1784 to train in the art of French cooking, and it was Hemings who brought macaroni and cheese—along with other classics like crème brûlée and French fries—back to America.

Once I learned that Hemings boiled his noodles in milk, I started doing the same, adding chicken stock for depth. Just a small tweak, but it made all the difference.

That's the thing about mac and cheese—it's the best when you make it your own. Measure with love, improvise with intention, and trust that what makes it delicious is the soul you stir into it.

INGREDIENTS

- 1 lb elbow macaroni
- 4 cups whole milk (use 2 cups for boiling + 2 cups for sauce)
- 2 cups chicken stock
- 1 stick butter (½ cup)
- ½ cup flour
- 1 cup each: sharp cheddar, Monterey Jack, mozzarella, Parmesan
- 1 cup evaporated milk
- 2 eggs, beaten
- Salt, pepper, paprika, garlic powder (measure with love)

MAKE IT

1. Cook macaroni in 2 cups milk + 2 cups chicken stock until just al dente. Drain lightly.
2. In a saucepan, melt butter. Whisk in flour to make a roux. Slowly add remaining milk and evaporated milk, whisking until smooth and thick.
3. Stir in most of the cheese, saving some for the topping. Season generously.
4. Combine pasta, sauce, and beaten eggs in a large bowl. Pour into a buttered baking dish.
5. Top with remaining cheese. Sprinkle paprika.
6. Bake at 375°F for 35–40 minutes until bubbly and golden at the edges.

SERVE HOT. This isn't side-dish mac—it's centerpiece mac. The kind that shows up at the table already blessed and leaves people whispering, *"Who made this?"*

PART IV
Narrative Is Inheritance

PLAYLIST

"FAMILY REUNION"	THE O'JAYS
"DANCE WITH MY FATHER"	LUTHER VANDROSS
"PAPA WAS A ROLLING STONE"	THE TEMPTATIONS
"JUST MY IMAGINATION"	THE TEMPTATIONS
"AND THE BEAT GOES ON"	THE WHISPERS

Key Lime Pie
(AKA SWEET & SHARP)

My dad and dessert go together. Always have. Always will.

One of my favorite memories is the two of us hiding in the garage with a box of warm Krispy Kremes, eating in silence like fugitives. Not because we were ashamed, but because neither of us wanted my stepmom, or his diabetes, to catch us. Stepmom? YAS, chile. A glorious one. But that's a whole other story for another book.

Anyway, dessert is his gateway to his inner child. The same boy who once stole a whole crate of bananas, dragged it into a closet, and ate himself sick. He still can't eat bananas to this day.

That's the thing about my dad: sweetness unlocks him. Key lime pie is his shorthand. He'll order it every single time it's on the menu. Polished, tart, sweet, a little mischievous. Just like him.

CRUST

- 1 ½ cups graham cracker crumbs
- ⅓ cup sugar
- 6 tbsp melted butter

FILLING

- 4 egg yolks
- 1 can (14 oz) sweetened condensed milk
- ½ cup key lime juice (fresh if possible)

TOPPING

- Whipped cream (homemade or store-bought, no judgment)

MAKE IT

1. Preheat the oven to 350°F.
2. Mix graham cracker crumbs, sugar, and melted butter. Press into a 9-inch pie pan. Bake for 10 minutes. Cool slightly.
3. In a bowl, whisk egg yolks, condensed milk, and lime juice until smooth. Pour into the crust.

4. Bake for 15–18 minutes, until tiny bubbles form on the surface.
5. Chill for at least 2 hours. Top with whipped cream.

SERVE CHILLED. Eat it with a fork and knife if you want to be fancy—or straight from the pan if you need comfort quick. Either way, it's a slice of sweet certainty in a world full of sharp edges.

PART V
The Messy In-Between

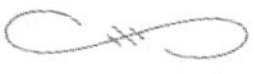

PLAYLIST

"WHAT YOU WON'T DO FOR LOVE" .... BOBBY CALDWELL

"WICKED GAMES" .... THE WEEKND

"I LIKE THAT" .... JANELLE MONAE

"6 INCH" .... BEYONCÉ

"GOOD DAYS" .... SZA

Spicy Shrimp Street Tacos

(AKA PERMISSION TO BE MESSY)

Nothing quite cures a hangover—or hits the spot after a long night of debauchery—like tacos. Specifically, the kind served from a truck parked in the sketchiest part of town, eaten standing up under a neon light.

But in the light of day, when both you and your taste buds have sobered up, spicy shrimp tacos elevate the experience. They're what you eat curled up on the couch, watching reality TV in yesterday's clothes, grateful for food that doesn't judge you.

Messy, delicious, and just spicy enough to keep things interesting—tacos are proof that sometimes what we need isn't polished or perfect. Sometimes we just need flavor, heat, and a little reminder that life is better when it drips down your wrist.

FOR THE SHRIMP

- 1 lb raw shrimp, peeled & deveined
- 1 tbsp olive oil
- 1 tsp smoked paprika
- 1 tsp chili powder
- ½ tsp cumin
- ½ tsp garlic powder
- Salt + pepper
- Juice of 1 lime

FOR THE SLAW

- 2 cups shredded cabbage
- ¼ cup mayo
- 1 tbsp hot honey (or honey + chili flakes)
- 1 tbsp apple cider vinegar
- Salt to taste

TO SERVE

- Small corn tortillas (lightly charred)
- Pickled red onions
- Avocado slices
- Fresh cilantro
- Lime wedges

MAKE IT

1. Toss shrimp with olive oil, spices, salt, pepper, and lime juice. Sauté for 2–3 minutes per side until pink and just cooked.
2. Mix cabbage, mayo, hot honey, and vinegar for a quick slaw.
3. Warm tortillas, then layer shrimp, slaw, pickled onions, and avocado. Top with cilantro and a squeeze of lime.

SERVE MESSY. These aren't polite tacos. Eat with your hands, let the sauce drip, and don't apologize. Life—like tacos—tastes better when you let yourself get a little bit dirty.

PART VI
The Return to Myself

PLAYLIST

"FLAWLESS (REMIX)" .... BEYONCÉ FT. NICKI MINAJ

"BAG LADY" .... ERYKAH BADU

"I AM LIGHT" .... INDIA.ARIE

"TRY" .... COLBIE CAILLAT

Grumbo

(AKA THAT GOOD, DEEP GUMBO)

My grandfather made gumbo. It always felt like a special occasion, because he didn't make it often. The ingredients varied depending on what was available, but the flavor never betrayed you. You could count on that rich, layered base—and then be surprised by whatever he decided to throw in. Oysters, sometimes. Always soul.

He was born in Texas, and his country roots were never far behind. On more than one occasion I'd open our deep freezer and find a possum or raccoon waiting inside—a silent warning to maybe avoid the protein coming out of the kitchen for a few days. But gumbo days were the exception. Nobody questioned the pot. Nobody asked. We just ate.

Honestly, who knows what was in his gumbo? I just know it tasted like home. And even as a kid, I knew it tasted like home to my grandpa too.

INGREDIENTS

- ¾ cup vegetable oil
- 1 cup all-purpose flour
- 1 ½ cups finely chopped onions
- ¾ cup finely chopped green bell peppers
- ¾ cup finely chopped celery
- 2 tbsp minced garlic
- One 12-ounce bottle amber beer
- 6 cups shrimp stock
- ¼ tsp dried thyme
- 2 bay leaves
- ½ lb gumbo crabs (about 2)
- 2 tsp Worcestershire sauce
- 1 ½ tsp salt
- ½ tsp cayenne pepper
- 1 lb medium shrimp, peeled and deveined
- 1 lb white fish fillets (catfish, grouper, snapper, or sole)
- 1 tbsp Creole seasoning
- 2 cups shucked oysters with their liquor
- ¼ cup chopped fresh parsley
- ½ cup chopped green onion tops
- White rice, for serving

MAKE IT

1. Heat oil in an 8-quart stockpot over medium heat for about 5 minutes. Stir in flour to form a roux. Lower heat to medium-low and stir constantly for 15–20 minutes, until the color of milk chocolate.
2. Add onions, bell peppers, and celery to the roux. Cook for 5 minutes, then stir in garlic. Cook 30 seconds more.
3. Add beer and shrimp stock, stirring to blend. Season with thyme, bay leaves, crabs, Worcestershire, salt, and cayenne. Bring to a boil, then lower to a simmer. Cook for 1 hour, skimming foam and oil from the surface.
4. Season shrimp and fish with Creole seasoning. Stir them into the gumbo and cook for 2 minutes.
5. Add oysters and cook 5 minutes more, stirring often.
6. Stir in parsley and green onions just before serving.

SERVE OVER WHITE RICE. Gumbo forgives—it adapts to whatever you've got, but it always brings people together. It's proof that home isn't about perfection. It's about a foundation strong enough to hold all your substitutions, surprises, and second chances.

PART VII
A Devotion to the Woman I Am

PLAYLIST

"LEVEL UP"	CIARA
"GOOD AS HELL"	LIZZO
"RISE UP"	ANDRA DAY
"COFFEE"	SYLVAN ESSO
"BLESSED"	JILL SCOTT

Fluffy Pancakes
(AKA SOFT RETURN)

I love pancakes. They are my ultimate comfort food—breakfast, lunch, or dinner. They're the friend I want to tell all my joys and sorrows to. There's no pancake vs. waffle debate for me. A waffle could never.

Pancakes are the food version of a soft place to land. They're circular and forgiving, stacked high like proof that there's always more waiting for you. A love letter made edible.

For a brief time in high school, I helped promote underground hip-hop shows with a crew of friends who loved the culture and the art. Tyson, brother in spirit, boss of me in his heart, was the resident MC and the kind of serious that made you trust anything that came out of his mouth. After shows, while most teenagers were finding new ways to get in trouble, we found pancakes.

We'd pile into IHOP for stacks and milkshakes, letting the night dissolve into something softer. Pancakes were punctuation, the return to wholesomeness, the literal soft place to land at the end of every story.

INGREDIENTS

- 1 cup all-purpose flour
- 1 tbsp sugar
- 1 tsp baking powder
- ½ tsp baking soda
- Pinch of salt
- 1 egg
- 1 cup buttermilk (or milk + 1 tsp vinegar/lemon juice)
- 2 tbsp melted butter
- 1 tsp vanilla (optional)

MAKE IT

1. Whisk dry ingredients in one bowl. In another, whisk egg, buttermilk, butter, and vanilla.
2. Stir wet into dry until just combined—lumps are welcome.

3. Let the batter rest 5–10 minutes while you heat a skillet or griddle.
4. Pour ¼ cup per pancake. Flip once bubbles form and edges look set. Cook until golden.

SERVE STACKED. With butter melting down the sides, syrup pooling at the bottom, and all the warmth of a love letter you can eat.

I'm not here to turn you into a chef. I'm here to remind you that joy is edible, that memory is seasoned, and that sometimes the holiest thing you can do is eat something messy with your hands while a song you love plays too loud.

Recipes are just stories you can taste. May they land on your tongue the way they landed on mine . . . unexpected, unruly, and exactly enough.

ACKNOWLEDGMENTS

I want to name them because saying their names out loud feels like a prayer.

My grandmother, Juanita. My mother, Candice. My aunts, Denise, Tina, Margo, Melinda, Carolyn, Arnita, Shermaine, who raised me loud and tender, with equal parts love and humor.

My sisters, Tanesha and Jaszmine.

My cousins, Miesha, Juanita, Ferris, JoJo, Kennedi.

My friends, Lauren, Lisa, Nora, Renee G., Renee B., Jessica O., and my forever work wife, Jessica (JP), proof that chosen family can be just as binding as blood.

My sons, Thaddaeus, Journey, Justice, and Jordan. My greatest teachers, my cherished friends, my joy in human form.

And to the men who guided me with patience and presence. My grandfather John. My father, William. My best friends, Cupid, Drew, Jemiah, Kelvin, Mike, Thomas, and Tyson. My uncle Sherman. My forever family, my ex-husband, Taijon.

To the first person who coached me and offered much-needed critical feedback, Judge Sharon Chatman. And to those who shaped me professionally, who gave me mentorship, friendship, and the space to be my authentic self so I could grow my talents in tech and creatively, Ryan Azus, Deji Odujinrin, Faiza Hugell, Eric Lewis, Kyle Wakefield, Jim Culkar, Art Harding, Emilie Dettamanti, Jez Medina, Kevin Williams, James Ettig, Trey Hornberger, Ashley Schwandt, Brian Power, and Lyndsey Fletcher.

To my editor, Anita Martin, my photographer, Renee Boccasile, my early readers, and the Amplify team, Kristin and Camma, thank you for shaping these pages with such care.

And to every person who has ever shared their own messy, beautiful truth with me. This book is stitched with you, too.

ABOUT THE AUTHOR

MYA FORT-MARSHALL is a writer, speaker, and truth-teller who believes in the power of story to heal and connect. A mom, cancer survivor, and sometimes pirate, she has built her career leading marketing and revenue growth for global tech companies—shaping strategies, building high-performing teams, and proving that resilience and authenticity belong both in the boardroom and at the kitchen table.

Her work blends memoir, philosophy, and culture—with humor as sharp as her survival skills. Mya is the founder of SoulDope, a nonprofit dedicated to bridging the opportunity gap through education and access to technology, and the creator of Wonder Purpose Soul, a platform for wonder, reflection, and truth-telling.

When she's not writing or speaking, you can find her laughing too loudly with her family, experimenting with recipes, or planning her next adventure. *Before You Were Everything* is her first book.